GOLD VALUE
and
GOLD PRICES
From 1971 - 2021

An Empirical Model

Gary Christenson

BALBOA.
PRESS

A DIVISION OF HAY HOUSE

Balboa Press books may be ordered through booksellers or by contacting:

Balboa Press
A Division of Hay House
1663 Liberty Drive
Bloomington, IN 47403
www.balboapress.com
1 (877) 407-4847

Because of the dynamic nature of the Internet, any web addresses or links contained in this book may have changed since publication and may no longer be valid. The views expressed in this work are solely those of the author and do not necessarily reflect the views of the publisher, and the publisher hereby disclaims any responsibility for them.

The author of this book does not dispense financial advice. The intent of the author is only to offer information of a general nature to help you in your quest for financial well-being.

Any people depicted in stock imagery provided by Thinkstock are models, and such images are being used for illustrative purposes only.
Certain stock imagery © Thinkstock.

Printed in the United States of America.

ISBN: 978-1-4525-1706-3 (sc)
ISBN: 978-1-4525-1707-0 (e)

Balboa Press rev. date: 06/24/2014

For Diana

CONTENTS

Part 3: Action Plans

LIST OF ILLUSTRATIONS

INTRODUCTION

We are all concerned about our savings, investments, income, and daily expenses. Most of us worry we will not have enough saved for retirement or perhaps not have enough cash to cover the next mortgage payment. We do our best in this complex financial and economic world, but most of us know that our understanding is limited. How do we improve our daily financial life and better manage our savings and investment plans?

Most people listen to experts. We trust that professionals know best and we assume we will benefit by following the advice and direction of professional money managers, doctors, accountants, financial planners, and other recognized experts.

But it is an unfortunate fact that professionals are often wrong, and that professionals with similar expertise often disagree.

It is a confusing world.

Our financial world is complex and further muddled by varying market perspectives, outright lies, government and central bank management, market manipulations, high frequency trading practices, and so much more.

In addition we are influenced by what is called normalcy bias whereby we assume that conditions in the future will be similar to present trends and conditions. This sometimes works but it spectacularly fails at important turning points in the markets. A few examples where normalcy bias was highly destructive:

a) Buying stocks in September 1929
b) Buying gold in early January 1980
c) Selling US stocks in 1982
d) Buying Japanese land and stocks in 1989
e) Buying internet stocks in January 2000
f) Selling gold in 2001
g) Buying Florida condominiums in 2006

Investing is difficult, but investing in gold is even more confusing because gold ownership has been discouraged for over 80 years, since 1933 when President Roosevelt declared a bank holiday and ordered U.S. citizens to hand over their gold to the government. Since 1971, when President Nixon formally terminated the agreement to exchange gold for dollars held by foreigners, the dollar has been backed by nothing more substantial than the full faith and credit of the U.S. government.

In fact, the dollars we currently use are debt based Federal Reserve Notes, which are liabilities of the private, banker owned, Federal Reserve Central Bank of the United States. The Federal Reserve and central banks around the world create and lend their dollars, euros, yen, and other paper currencies while discouraging trust in gold. Objectively speaking, we should not look to central bankers for unbiased analysis regarding the value of gold because central bankers view gold as a competitor to their debt based paper currencies.

But where should we look for sensible, unbiased, and rational analysis of the gold market? Who and what should we believe regarding gold, its value, and its place in our saving and investment plans?

I believe we should discount most statements from central bankers, remain skeptical of political agendas, and trust the wisdom gleaned from 5,000 years of market history. That wisdom suggests that in early 2014, as this is written, gold is an excellent choice for financial insurance, secure savings, and as a long term investment that protects from further currency devaluation.

HOW DO WE DETERMINE A FAIR VALUE FOR GOLD?

Answer: Create an empirical model for gold prices that determines long term value based on other macro-economic variables! This is NOT a trading model. It is an investing model that calculates a "fair" or equilibrium value for gold to help determine when we should purchase gold and what gold prices we can reasonably expect several years into the future.

A real world example: We want to drive to a park, spread a blanket on the grass, and have a picnic with our favorite foods and beverages. What preparations would we make?

- Examine the weather forecast for the day of our picnic.
- Plan the menu.
- Check the roadmap to make certain we know the route to the park.

Investing Example: We have money to invest. What preparations should we make?

- Determine what investments should receive our investment dollars such as growth stocks, dividend stocks, money market funds, gold bullion, silver coins, diamonds, farmland and so forth.
- Examine appropriate ratios such as Price to Earnings ratios to determine if these investments seem overpriced or represent good value as investments.

- Check the history and trends for these investments and determine if they appear to be near cyclic lows or cyclic highs, and how we can reasonably expect them to perform in the future.
- Consider the larger trends established by our governments and central banks. Are governments inflating the money supply, spending irresponsibly, and accelerating consumer price inflation, or have our governments and central bankers become more responsible and accountable in their political and economic policies?

Stocks, bonds and real estate have been extensively analyzed in many ways, including ratios and other comparisons, but we have few generally understood tools for a proper valuation of gold. This is an important reason why we need a model for gold prices that will determine if gold is currently overpriced or underpriced, and if the future of gold looks bleak or bright.

The model should function like a roadmap. We are more secure traveling from point A to point B if we have a roadmap. Similarly, if we have a model for the valuation of gold, we will be more confident in our long term investment decisions regarding the purchase or sale of gold.

So, I created an empirical model!

PART 1

THE GOLD EMPIRICAL MODEL – A GEM

Part 1 explores the need for an empirical model, examines gold prices since 1971, smoothed gold prices, the macro-economic variables used in the model, the actual formula that replicates smoothed gold prices, and future gold prices as projected by the model.

Part 1 also discusses gold cycles, various ratios, and shows how those cycles and ratios support the price projections from the Gold Empirical Model (GEM).

CHAPTER 1

EXPERTS WHO DON'T AGREE

GOLD AS WEALTH:

For thousands of years an ounce of gold was just that – an ounce of gold – and a significant amount of wealth or savings. But man invented paper money and digital currencies, confused paper with wealth, increased the supply of paper money, created price inflation, and consequently the value of paper currencies decreased, and that forced the price of gold much higher.

The important question has changed from "How much gold do you own?" to "How many paper dollars does it take to buy an ounce of gold?"

HOW DO WE DETERMINE AN APPROPRIATE PRICE FOR AN OUNCE OF GOLD?

1) GOLD AND DEBT:

Jim Sinclair calculated a possible extreme value for gold based on the external US debt and the quantity of gold supposedly held by the U.S. Government and the Federal Reserve at Fort Knox and other official depositories.

His calculation was:

- Take 90% of the total international dollar debt, not including debt to China, add 50% of the debt to China, and then divide by the amount of gold officially held by the United States. The result is increasing every day as the total external debt continually expands. The question as to how much gold actually remains in the official vaults and is neither leased nor sold is unanswered, but we will speculate on that topic later.
- The answer, as of April 2014, is a potential value for gold in the range of $12,000 to $15,000 per ounce. One might be tempted to dismiss this calculation as unrealistic but a similar calculation made by Mr. Sinclair in the early 1970s came very close to predicting the 1980 high in gold at about $850 per ounce.

2) GOLD AND BANKERS:

Bankers deal with debt and currency all their lives. One might expect that they would have informed opinions regarding the value and price of gold. What have bankers stated about gold?

- In testimony to Congress in 1912, JP Morgan has been quoted as saying, *"Gold is money. Everything else is credit."* He should know.
- Paul Volcker, the Chairman of the Federal Reserve from 1979 – 1987, supposedly stated, *"Gold is my enemy."* As you know the dollar was being printed in excess during the 1960s and 1970s to finance the Vietnam War and new social programs. From 1970 to 1980 the price of gold moved from about $42 per ounce to over $800 per ounce. Mr. Volcker's statement is understandable when viewed from the perspective of a central banker desperately trying to maintain confidence in the dollar and convince the world that the unbacked dollar was still a viable currency and a store of value.

- Benjamin Bernanke, Chairman of the Federal Reserve in 2013, stated, *"Nobody really understands gold prices and I don't pretend to understand them either."*
- Janet Yellen, current Chairman of the Federal Reserve, stated in 2013 *"I don't think anybody has a very good model of what makes gold prices go up or down…"*

Since the main "product" of the Federal Reserve is unbacked debt based currency, Federal Reserve Notes, we should expect the Federal Reserve to discourage the understanding of gold, its importance as a store of value, and as a measure of dollar weakness.

Note: The Federal Reserve currently employs about 17,000 employees, many of whom are highly intelligent analysts with PhDs. The Federal Reserve has access to an immense amount of current and historical data and owns massive computing capacity, yet officially, nobody understands gold prices. I find this … interesting.

3) GOLD AND THE MONEY SUPPLY:

James Turk related the value of gold to the money supply through his concept of a "fear index." His formula is:

$$\text{Fear Index} = \frac{\text{US Gold Reserves x Gold's Market Price}}{\text{M3}}$$

The Fear Index has ranged from approximately 1% to 7.5% over the past 42 years and is currently near its lows. James Turk thinks that bank solvency is questionable and sovereign debts cannot be repaid. Hence he believes the fear index and the price of gold will increase substantially from their current low levels.

4) EXPERT OPINIONS REGARDING GOLD:

There are many other estimates, opinions, and projections. See the notes at the end of the book for additional opinions and projections.

- Harry Dent is a well-known demographer. His assessment is that commodities and specifically gold will decline in price due to demographic forces around the world. His published target for gold is $750 and possibly much lower.
- Robert Prechter is a well-known Elliott Wave analyst who sees gold falling, due to overwhelming deflationary forces, well below $1,000 and perhaps to $400 in the next several years.
- David Marotta is a Certified Financial Planner with an interesting interpretation on gold. He states that *"the optimal allocation to gold is always zero because its return is too low to be a real investment ..."*
- Martin Armstrong has an encyclopedic knowledge of history, economics, and money. He will not be surprised if gold drops below $1,000 in 2014 and thereafter rallies substantially higher as fiat dollars plummet in purchasing power.
- Jim Sinclair, often known as Mr. Gold, has half a century of experience in the gold and financial markets. In 2001 he made the incredible (at that time) prediction that gold would rise to $1,650 by the 3rd week of January in 2011. At the time of his prediction gold was selling for less than $300. His prediction was off a bit; gold surpassed $1,650 in August of 2011, a few months later than his 10 year old prediction. Impressive! Since then Mr. Sinclair has publicly stated that gold will rise to $3,500 on its way to much higher prices, depending on weakness in the dollar and the amount of Quantitative Easing, otherwise known as injecting liquidity, bond monetization, or "money printing". He has suggested that $10,000 or more is possible.
- James Rickards is a well-known author and economist. His latest book, "The Death of Money: The Coming Collapse of the

International Monetary System" was published in April 2014. He stated that we should expect a gold price of $7,000 to $10,000. See the notes at the end for his calculations.

My point is that highly intelligent, experienced, and well-known experts disagree substantially. **In fact they cannot even agree as to whether gold is likely to trade higher or lower in the next three years.** At the time of this writing gold is selling for approximately $1,300 on the COMEX, the primary market for gold and silver in the United States. If experts project gold somewhere between $400 and $10,000 in the next three to seven years, then I believe that we need something more objective and defensible than the opinions of experts, regardless of how intelligent and experienced.

We need an objective model to project the value of gold. We need a model that bypasses the propaganda, self-serving forecasts, market manipulations, media disinformation, and the influence of high frequency trading to "manage" the gold market.

We need a simple and understandable empirical model for gold prices based on macro-economic variables that are relatively easy to measure and project several years into the future.

CHAPTER 2

GOLD PRICES - THE LAST 42 YEARS

Like most markets the price of gold has been volatile during the past 42 years. However, the upward trend is unmistakable. Consider the following graph of monthly gold prices since 1971.

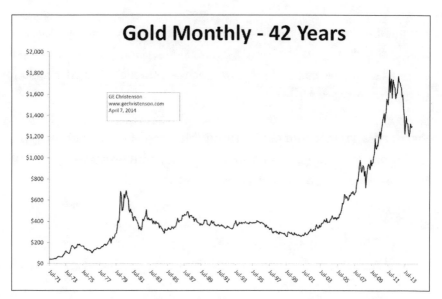

Now examine this graph of monthly gold prices over the past 10 years.

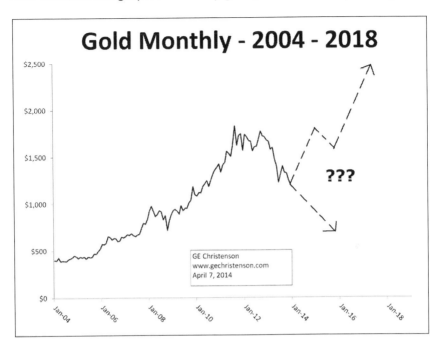

I have drawn an arrow showing an upward trend and a second arrow depicting a downward trend. The question is: Will gold reverse its short term down trend and rally during 2014 and subsequent years, or will it continue its down trend toward lower prices?

Examine the longer term chart of gold again. There have been periods of time when gold prices fell – such as from 1980 to 2001. Was the peak in 1980 similar to the peak in 2011 or radically different? There are differing opinions, which is another reason why we need a model that provides a more objective evaluation of gold prices.

Now examine the price of gold after it has been smoothed as follows:

Each monthly price was smoothed with a 13 month centered moving average. Example: the smoothed price for July 1987 gold was the simple average of all the monthly prices from January 1987 through January 1988. To create an annual smoothed gold price, the monthly smoothed prices for January – December of each year were averaged. The result was a smoothed gold price as shown in the following graph.

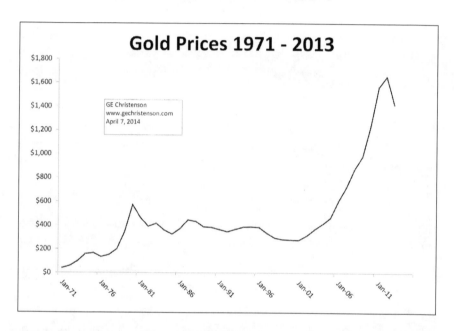

However, to further smooth the gold price, I took the annual prices, as calculated above, and smoothed them with a three year centered moving average. Example: the additionally smoothed 1987 gold price was the average of the smoothed 1986, 1987 and 1988 gold prices.

That further smoothed gold price graph is shown here.

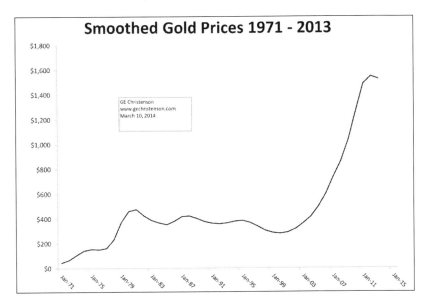

In the smoothed graph the strong upward bias is clear.

Now examine that same data plotted on a logarithmic scale which shows the exponential increase.

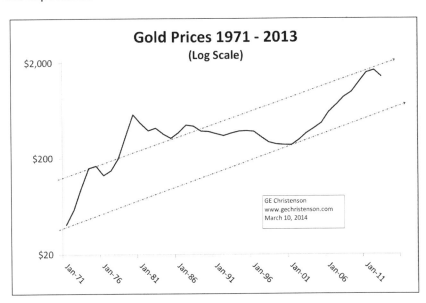

CHAPTER 3

MODEL GUIDELINES AND VARIABLES

This chapter explores the guidelines that I consider important in the creation of a model. Further, I discuss many possible macro-economic variables and choose only a few.

Model Guidelines:

- Replicate the smoothed prices for gold since President Nixon closed the "gold window" on August 15, 1971. By executive order he announced that the United States would no longer exchange foreign owned dollars for gold. His action enabled the reduction in value and purchasing power of the dollar through massive inflation of the money supply.
- Use inputs that are easy to identify, measure, and are intuitively sensible in their causal relationship to gold prices.
- Use inputs that can be projected into the future with some degree of confidence.
- Keep it simple and easy to understand. A simple model is more credible and less susceptible to "curve-fitting" that forces agreement with the smoothed gold price.
- Calculate an equilibrium or "fair" market value for gold prices that has been smoothed to filter out the noise, short-term manipulations, high frequency trading distortions, political pressures, and temporary supply and demand changes.

- Do NOT attempt to predict weekly or monthly gold market prices.
- Do NOT use past or current gold prices to predict future gold prices.
- Do NOT expect perfection.

VARIABLES USED IN THE MODEL:

Many macro-economic variables could be used as inputs to a gold model. Examples are:

- The CPI, the consumer price index.
- Japanese Yen
- Swiss Franc
- 30 year T-bond yield
- 10 year T-note yield
- National Debt (official)
- Fed Funds Rate
- M2 (a measure of money supply)
- M3 (a discontinued measure of money supply)
- TMS – the True Money Supply – a measure of money supply advocated by the "Austrian" school of economics
- Real interest rates – the short term interest rate less the current inflation rate
- U.S. Dollar index
- Silver prices
- Copper prices
- Crude Oil prices
- S&P 500 Index
- Dow Jones Industrial Average
- Many more

The price of gold is probably related to each of these macro-economic variables. For example:

- M2, M3, TMS: As more currency is printed into circulation, the value of each unit, whether it be dollars, euros, or yen, falls. As the value or purchasing power of each unit declines, the prices of gold, food, energy, and most commodities rise.
- Real Interest rates: As real interest rates rise the demand for financial assets increases and the demand for hard assets generally decreases. Broadly speaking the period from 1980 – 2001 was a time of increasing demand for financial assets and consequently it was a bear market period for gold and silver.
- The Dollar Index: As the dollar rises, on average, gold falls. When the Yen, Euro, and Swiss Franc rise the dollar falls, and gold rises.
- National Debt: As government spends in excess of its revenues the national debt rises and more dollars are created and spent into circulation. The national debt correlates closely with the various measures such as M2, M3, and the TMS. Broadly speaking, as the national debt increases, the purchasing power of the dollar decreases and the price of gold increases.

I have tested many of these macro-economic variables and found that some are highly correlated with the price of gold, some move oppositely to the price of gold, and some are weakly correlated. A good model identifies the important variables and optimizes their weighting to accurately replicate the smoothed price of gold.

OTHER VARIABLES:

If I suggested that Japanese rice production, Alaskan salmon catch, or congressional approval ratings should be used in the model, you might be skeptical. I can think of no relationship between Japanese rice production or the Alaskan salmon catch that should affect the price of gold. It is possible that congressional approval ratings are inversely related to the price of gold but I doubt the relationship is clear or reliable.

More importantly, even if Japanese rice production over the past 42 years were a near perfect fit with the price of gold, I would not use it to project gold prices. If I can't determine a causal relationship between rice production and gold, I would not trust rice production to accurately project future gold prices.

In conclusion, I used variables that are logically connected with the price of gold and optimized their weighting to create a model that accurately replicates the smoothed price of gold. If the model worked well for many years in the past over a variety of political and monetary conditions, we can reasonably expect it to work, under mostly similar conditions, in the future.

CHAPTER 4

THE MODEL USES MACRO-ECONOMIC VARIABLES

Most of the variables listed in chapter 3 were tested in earlier versions of the model. After extensive testing I simplified the model to include only three variables.

The 1st variable is the official national debt:

Examine the graph of the official national debt (www.treasurydirect.gov) from 1971 – 2013.

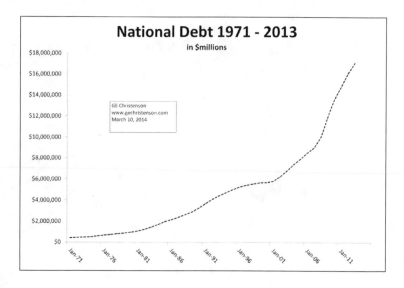

National Debt 1971 - 2013
in $millions

GE Christenson
www.gechristenson.com
March 10, 2014

Year		Official Debt
1971	(6/30/1971)	$398 Billion
2013	(9/30/2013)	$16,738 Billion (nearly $17 Trillion)

Yes, the official national debt as of September 30, 2013 was nearly $17 Trillion, or nearly $17,000 Billion. The national debt exponentially increased from 1971 to 2013 at an annually compounded rate of 9.25%. Since September 30, 2001 the exponential rate of increase has been 9.22%. Since September 30, 2008 the rate has been 10.8%. As you can see, the increase in national debt caused by expenditures in excess of U.S. government revenues has been remarkably consistent at 9 to 11% per year. If we assume the rate of increase since September 30, 2008 continuing into the future, the official national debt could exceed $30 Trillion by 2021.

Based on the retiring of baby-boomers, increased health and pension expenses for an aging population, and the weakening economy which will hurt government revenues, we have every reason to expect deficits will increase and that the national debt probably will increase more rapidly than 10 - 11% per year.

The next graph shows national debt and the smoothed price of gold since 1971. As you can see the graphs are similar when viewed over the 42 year period.

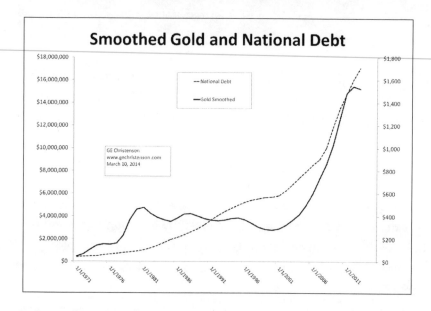

The next graph shows the same data for the smoothed gold price and the national debt but on a log scaled chart. In this chart a move from $1 Trillion to $2 Trillion is the same size on the chart as a move from $4 Trillion to $8 Trillion. This chart shows the exponential growth in the national debt and the smoothed price of gold.

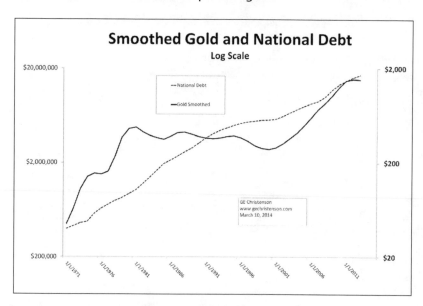

Obviously an exponential growth rate will not last forever. At some point other factors will restrict the growth or crash the system. How long the exponential growth can continue is impossible to answer, and many individuals have been forecasting a systemic collapse for some time. However the system has endured and may continue for a few more years or perhaps a few more decades. The exponentially growing national debt correlates well with smoothed gold. The correlation was 0.89 from 1971 – 2013.

The 2ⁿᵈ Variable is Crude Oil:

Examine the next graph of smoothed gold and the price of crude oil, also smoothed with the same process used for gold prices. As you can see the graphs are generally similar. From 1971 – 1980 both gold and crude were in bull markets. From 1980 to the late 1990s for crude and to 2001 for gold, both were in bear markets. A simple characterization of that roughly 20 year period of time was that financial assets were in substantial demand and commodities were not in favor. During that time the S&P 500 Index increased by about a factor of 13 while both gold and crude lost over half of their 1980 price.

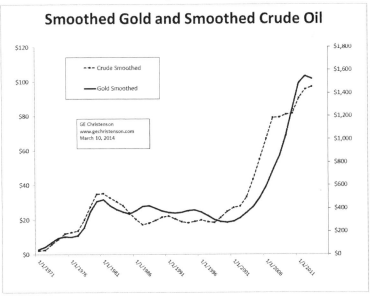

The correlation between the price of smoothed gold and smoothed crude oil over this 42 year period was about 0.92. Graphically you can see that gold acted like other commodities and fell out of favor, along with crude, during the years from about 1980 to 2001. Since then both gold and crude have risen substantially.

Year	Crude	High/Low	Year	Gold
1998	$10.75	Lows	2001	$255
2008	$147	Highs	2011	$1,900

Crude oil prices took 9.5 years and rose by a factor of 13.5 from bottom to top, while gold prices took 10 years and rose by a factor of 7.5.

Subsequent to these dramatic price rises the price of crude oil crashed by about 75% in five months and gold fell by nearly 40% in 2.5 years. After the crash low in crude oil in late 2008 at about $35 it has since risen to approximately $100 as of March 2014.

The 3rd Variable is the S&P 500 Index:

The 3rd variable is less intuitively obvious than the national debt and the price of crude oil. Think of the S&P 500 Index (S&P) as a competing investment to gold and other commodities. When the S&P is strongly in demand, such as from 1982 – 2000 the commodities are out of favor. Similarly the S&P peaked in 1966 and bottomed about 16 years later in 1982, while those years were strongly positive for gold and most commodities.

In the longer term both gold and the S&P are likely to rise since they are measured in dollars which continue to shrink in purchasing power. While the multi-decade trend for both gold and the S&P is up, their shorter term trends are opposite. Over a period of several years we can expect that if gold is rising, on average, the S&P will be under pressure. A good example of this is the period from August 2007 to March 2008 when the price of gold rallied over 50% and the S&P fell by about 15%. Similarly from August 2011 to December 2013 the price of gold fell by nearly 40% while the S&P rose by over 50%.

The next graph shows smoothed gold and the S&P 500 Index. Both moved erratically higher during the 42 year period from 1971. However, their short term movements were often opposite from each other.

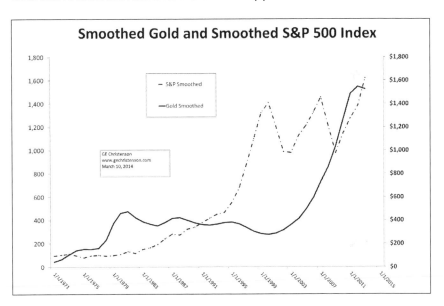

SUMMARY:

Gold and the national debt have moved dramatically higher over the past 42 years. National debt has increased exponentially by about 9 - 11% per year.

I also determined from the spreadsheet model that the annual rate of increase in the national debt was important. For example, if the national debt were rapidly increasing due to excessive expenditures or weak government revenues, the price of gold tended to increase more rapidly.

Gold and Crude Oil have both moved similarly, on average, in the past 42 years.

Gold and the S&P 500 Index have both moved upward, on average, in the past 42 years but they have moved, more or less, oppositely in the shorter term.

CHAPTER 5

THE EMPIRICAL FORMULA USED IN THE MODEL

A gold model should function accurately and consistently during all conditions in the financial markets. In other words, it should be accurate and effective during gold bull markets and gold bear markets, during stable and unstable political conditions, and during stock and bond market crashes and rallies.

Predicting daily gold prices is like predicting the weather – often not difficult for tomorrow, more difficult for next week, and quite difficult three months into the future. There are too many variables and apparently random occurrences, not to mention outright "management" by central banks, large traders, governments, and other powerful interests.

I believe that daily and weekly prices cannot be accurately and consistently predicted. Consequently I abandoned that essentially impossible project, and attempted to predict an average, "fair," or equilibrium price for smoothed gold market prices, understanding that actual market prices will occasionally spike higher or crash lower.

Hence my goal was the replication of the smoothed gold price with the short term volatility removed. The model is based on a formula that works under all market conditions and is intellectually honest. By that I mean:

- The formula is constant over all conditions. I would not use one formula during bull markets and a different formula during bear markets.
- The formula is based on real data without presuming an input that can't be measured. Example: The gold market seemed weak over a particular three year period so I added a "manipulation" factor of 13% for those three years and assume it was due to central bank sales of gold to the bullion banks. With a few such adjustments, I can create a model that has a near perfect match and little credibility. What adjustment will you presume for the year 2016? Hence the model must use actual data and exclude subjective adjustments in order to maintain intellectual credibility and honesty.
- The formula will inevitably produce a projected gold value that is occasionally too high or too low. Such short term moves are not important. However, it is important that the trend of the model matches the general trend of actual smoothed gold prices over the entire 42 year period. I expect to see model results that start low in 1971, rise to a peak in the early 1980s, fall erratically until about the year 2001, and generally rise to the end of the data – January 2014.
- Further, I expect that the statistical correlation between the calculated equilibrium gold price and the smoothed gold market price should be high. Ideal correlation is 1.00 so any correlation approaching 0.99 is excellent confirmation that the model has met my goals.

Variable Summary:

- Gold rises with the national debt.
- Gold rises and falls with the price of crude oil.

- Gold rises and falls in the short term (a few years) opposite to the direction of the S&P 500 Index.
- Gold is affected by the rate of change of the national debt – a more rapid increase in the national debt indicates a more rapid increase in the price of gold.

The formula can be created either arithmetically (adding weighted variables) or multiplicatively (multiplying weighted variables), or using both. I have tried many combinations and the best one that I have found is this:

EGP (Equilibrium Gold Price) =
$$\frac{K \times (ND)^a \times (CL)^b \times (ND\text{-}ROC)^d}{(SP)^c}$$

Where: ND = US National Debt in $ Millions
CL = Crude Oil in $ / 10
ND-ROC = Annual rate of change of the ND
SP = S&P 500 Index / 100

For example:

- The national debt is approximately $17 Trillion so ND = 17,000,000 Million
- The price of crude oil is approximately $102, so CL = $102/10 = 10.2
- The annual rate of change of the national debt is approximately 10% per year, so ND-ROC = 1.10
- The S&P 500 Index is currently about 1,800, so SP = 1800/100 = 18

In words the formula says:

> The equilibrium gold price is approximately equal to the product of a constant "K" times the national debt raised to the power of "a" times the price of crude oil raised to the power of "b" times the rate of change of the national debt raised to the power of "d" and all divided by the S&P 500 Index raised to the power of "c."

The formula calculates the equilibrium gold price using a plus one year offset. For example, the equilibrium gold price for 1998 is based on the 1997 values for national debt and its rate of change, crude oil, and the S&P 500 Index.

Obviously the five constants are crucial in determining the equilibrium gold price and the overall reliability and credibility of the model. To optimize the graphical similarity between the calculated and actual gold prices and to maximize the statistical correlation I tested hundreds of combinations of those five constants.

My experience suggests that it is very difficult to find the single best combination of numbers for those five constants. However, this combination worked quite well:

$K = 0.51$
$a = 0.41$ (national debt exponent)
$b = 0.90$ (crude oil exponent)
$c = 0.36$ (S&P 500 exponent)
$d = 2.00$ (rate of change of national debt exponent)

CHAPTER 6

RESULTS FROM
THE MODEL

The statistical correlation over a 42 year period between the smoothed equilibrium gold price and the smoothed market price of gold was 0.98 – quite good.

Examine the next graph of the actual smoothed gold price and the calculated or equilibrium gold price. Note the general trend similarities, along with deviations during the 1980s after the bubble in gold prices in 1979 – 1980, and the subsequent crash.

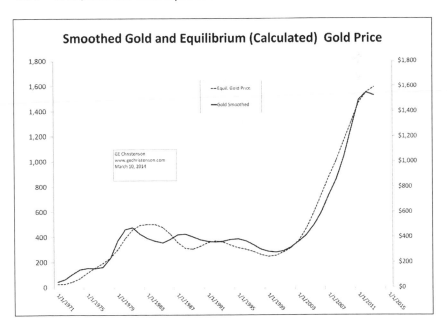

Graph Notes:

- Smoothed gold prices are shown with a solid line.
- Calculated equilibrium gold prices are shown with a dashed line.
- The long-term trend for gold prices was up from 1971 – 1980, down to 2001, and up since then. The calculated chart is similar in form to the smoothed price of gold.

I also used the same variables, national debt, price of crude oil, and the S&P 500 index, and attempted to model the price of gold in euros. Since all the inputs were US oriented variables, it is not surprising that the model was somewhat less successful in matching the price of gold expressed in euros. Further there were 42 years of relevant history with the dollar and only 15 years with the euro. However, given those limitations, the model created a generally accurate representation of gold priced in euros. See the graph below.

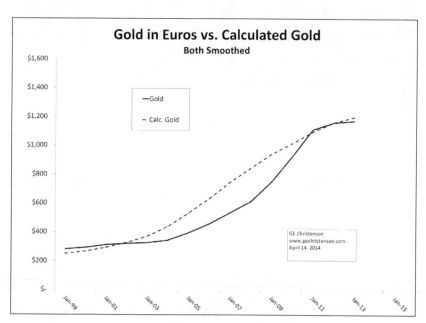

Why does this very simple model work so well?

- President Nixon "temporarily" closed the "gold window" on August 15, 1971. This removed any semblance of gold backing for the US Dollar, and more importantly, allowed dollars to be created in practically unlimited quantities. Since dollars are created as debt, the total debt in the system has exploded higher over the past 42 years, both in total dollars of debt and as a percentage of GDP. Total credit market debt divided by GDP is triple what it was 60 years ago and half again as large as its previous peak in 1933. The US economy has expanded while debt has grown much faster.

- Consequently the various measures of money supply, such as M2, M3, and TMS (True Money Supply) have increased exponentially since 1971.

- The prices for most commodities have also risen exponentially since 1971. Since many more dollars have been placed into circulation each dollar bought less, and the prices for food, energy, and housing have increased.

- Similarly the prices for the Dow Index and the S&P 500 Index have gone up sharply since each dollar was less valuable and that increased the nominal value of those stock indexes.

- The model is telling us what we all know – the money supply is increasing as we create more dollars – as indicated by the national debt exponentially increasing. Gold acts, to some degree, like a commodity, so it moves up and down along with the most important commodity in the world, crude oil. Occasionally gold, commodities, and hard assets are more desired, such as from 2001 - 2011, and occasionally financial assets are more desired, such as from 1982 – 2000. During those times when financial assets are in favor gold fares poorly and the S&P streaks higher.

- The model quantifies those broad trends of increasing debt, dollar debasement, and the varying desire for commodities versus financial assets.

THE MODEL IS ROBUST:

The model replicated smoothed gold prices over a 42 year period of difficult and erratic monetary, fiscal, and political conditions. Over those years we have experienced:

- Gold bull and bear markets.
- Stock bull and bear markets.
- Bond bear market and a bull market.
- Stock market crashes (1987, 2000, and 2008).
- Stock market bubble (Nasdaq in 1999 – 2000).
- Gold bubble (1979 – 1980).
- Volatile oil prices. The price in 1999 was under $11, peaked in 2008 at $147, and then fell to about $35.
- Quantitative Easing, "injecting liquidity," "money printing," and bond monetization.
- "Operation Twist" in which the Federal Reserve reduced long term interest rates.
- ZIRP or the Zero Interest Rate Policy in which the Federal Reserve reduced short term interest rates to near zero for a number of years.
- Y2K and 9-11.
- Shock and awe and various military invasions.
- Irrational exuberance in stocks, bonds, housing, gold, silver and crude oil prices.
- Cold wars, hot wars, and occasional peace.
- Democratic and republican presidents.
- Recessions and economic booms.

IMPORTANT NUMBERS:

- Gold was priced about 30% ABOVE the equilibrium gold price (EGP) in August of 2011 at the all-time high. The model indicated that the market price for gold at that time was too high and that an upcoming period of price weakness was probable – which occurred.

- Gold was priced about 26% BELOW the EGP in December of 2013 at what appears to have been a double-bottom low. The model indicated that given the size of the national debt, its rate of increase, the price of crude oil, and the price for the S&P 500 Index, the next large move for gold was much more likely to be up from that low in December 2013. At the time of this writing, that projected move up appears to be in progress.
- Statistical correlation over the 42 year period was 0.98.
- The actual gold market high price in 1980 exceeded the EGP by almost 100%. This is not surprising since, in retrospect, gold prices had clearly gone parabolic in a bubble blow-off rally during 1979 – 1980.
- Actual gold market prices dipped as much as 40% below the EGP at various times following the gold high in 1980. Markets that overshoot reasonable prices on the way up often crash to unsustainably low prices subsequent to those bubble highs.
- One standard deviation was calculated at about 25% of the EGP over the 42 year period. Assuming the standard bell-curve distribution, about 95% of market prices should lie within 50%, above or below, the equilibrium gold price. Fifty percent deviation above or below is a very broad range and allows for considerable volatility. Note: I have not confirmed that the data is fairly represented by a standard bell-curve of normal statistical distribution, but have made the unproven assumption that it is a "normal" distribution.

POSSIBLE CONCERNS REGARDING FUTURE PROJECTIONS:

- The future will not precisely fit the past. We live in interesting and dangerous times that, subjectively speaking, seem to be changing more rapidly. The model was robust and fairly represented smoothed gold prices during a very large range of unusual circumstances. However, there is no guarantee that the model will continue to accurately replicate the smoothed gold price.

- Currency wars, in which countries devalue their own currencies to increase exports, can have a dramatic impact upon foreign exchange rates, the value of currencies, and gold prices. Over the last century all currencies have devalued against gold and there is little reason to expect that ongoing trend to change. What is more important is the possibility that the US Dollar, the reserve currency of the world, might lose its status and devalue substantially against other currencies. Do not exclude the possibility of a panic exit from the dollar, a violent devaluation in the dollar against other currencies, and a concurrent upward revaluation in the price of gold. Some credible analysis argues this loss of reserve currency status is mathematically inevitable.

- So called "black swans" could dramatically change the nature of our political and monetary world. As I write Russia has troops on the border of the Ukraine and politicians are calling the Ukrainian situation a "crisis" and potentially the beginning of WWIII. Other events could affect the model projections. However the model might effectively handle all such events, short of a total economic collapse.

- The model was "curve fit" so the values used for the exponents in the model may work less effectively in the future.

"BLACK SWANS:"

By definition "black swans" are unpredictable and bring significant change to our political, economic and social worlds. The model projections might be highly effective in some circumstances and perhaps not in others. Regardless, I think it is important to consider some potentially world changing events.

Examples:

- China and Japan declare war upon each other due to South China Sea conflicts and both the United States and Russia enter into the war as combatants.
- A nuclear bomb destroys a major oil port in Saudi Arabia.
- Hyperinflation of the US dollar is established as unofficial policy to deal with exploding debts and entitlement expenses.
- An event, "false flag" or otherwise, brings the world to a limited nuclear war.

Other examples of unlikely but world changing events:

- The US congress reduces spending well below the current revenues and sincerely agrees to pay down the national debt to zero over the next 20 years.
- Convincing peace and political harmony are established in the middle-east and northern Africa.

While I consider an escalation of war and armed conflict far more likely, fiscal and monetary sanity and world peace are possible.

I have read that in 1913 the possibility of war in Europe was widely dismissed as extremely unlikely due to the existing prosperity and the wide-spread recognition that no country would benefit from war. As demonstrated in 1914, unlikely is not impossible, and "black swans" or other apparently insane events can and do occur.

Armed conflict and new wars are important to consider because, aside from devastation and disruption, they almost certainly will involve more debts, an escalation in the price of crude oil, and stock market weakness. As projected by the formula all three variables will propel the price of gold much higher. Further, there could be other collateral damage to world economics, currencies, and the hegemonic superiority of the United States. Specifically, it is not difficult to imagine global confidence in the dollar weakening due to massive borrowing, printing, and spending in another war effort.

The discussion of increased armed conflict and new wars is not merely academic. Many analysts have researched war cycles. Their research indicates that the likelihood of armed conflict and new wars increases substantially between 2013 and 2021. An internet search will produce many graphs of war cycles. Consider the impact of another war upon the prices for gold, crude, and other food and energy commodities.

CHAPTER 7

GOLD PRICES PROJECTED INTO THE FUTURE

The model tells us that smoothed gold prices can be approximated by three variables: official national debt, price of crude oil, and the S&P 500 index. We do not know what those prices will be in three years, but we can make reasonable assumptions.

National Debt: The national debt has grown consistently since 1913 when the Federal Reserve was established.

Year		Debt
1913	$3	Billion
1971	$398	Billion
2013	$16,738	Billion or nearly $17 Trillion

The annually compounded rate of increase from 1913 to 2013 has been about 9.0%. The annually compounded rate of increase from 1971 to 2013 has been about 9.25%. The rate of increase under the current administration, September 30, 2008 – September 30, 2013, has been about 10.8%.

It is reasonable to assume that retiring baby boomers and rapidly increasing Medicare and Medicaid costs will boost the deficit and thereby accelerate the rate of increase in the national debt. Further, any future wars, and many seem likely, will also accelerate the increase in the national debt. Assume national debt increases about 11 - 12% per year for the next decade.

Crude Oil Prices: It seems clear that the world is running out of inexpensive oil, more vehicles are driving more miles throughout the world, especially in Asia, and the world-wide demand for crude oil will grow. Hence the prices for crude oil are likely to increase during the next decade. The annual rate of increase over the past 14 years, January 1, 2000 to January 1, 2014 has been about 10.2%. Assume that crude oil increases about 10 - 12% per year for the next decade.

S&P 500 Index: I find it difficult to estimate the S&P 500 Index over the next five years. Some analysts see substantial drops while others assume continued growth in the S&P 500 based on the Federal Reserve policies, Quantitative Easing, ZIRP, and the desire to subsidize the financial industry. Assume that the S&P 500, which is near all-time highs, will remain constant or drop a small amount during the next decade.

Given those assumptions, and remembering that the market price for gold can easily spike above or below the EGP for months at a time, these estimates seem reasonable:

Year	EGP	Possible Spike Highs
2017	$2,400 - $2,900	$3,500 - $4,500
2021	$4,000 - $5,000	$6,000 - $8,000

Implicit in these projections are the following assumptions:

- These macro-economic variables continue to increase and decrease as they have for the past 42 years.
- The U.S. economy continues along its typical, but weakening, path with government expenses growing more rapidly than

revenues, as they have for decades. National debt rises inevitably as the government budget is never balanced, and "budget cuts" only mean reductions in the rate of increase of expenditures, but never an actual reduction in expenditures.

- Congress continues its multi-decade habit of borrowing and spending, talking about fiscal responsibility and change, but actually changes little and almost never eliminates or reduces a government program.
- The Federal Reserve supports the stock and bond markets and continues "liquidity injections," Quantitative Easing, and other monetary manipulations to support banks and the political and financial elite of the country.
- Monetary, political, and fiscal policies will NOT be materially different from what they have been during the past 42 years.
- The United States will NOT be subjected to global nuclear war, Weimar hyperinflation, or an economic collapse. However, the lower and middle classes will continue to suffer under the destructive policies of our current Keynesian economic nonsense.

CHAPTER 8

GOLD PRICES ARE MANAGED AND MANIPULATED

Global bankers have admitted to manipulating the LIBOR rates, which increased already massive profits for bankers from the multi-trillions of loans that are affected by the LIBOR rates.

The London Gold Pool was created to maintain the price of gold within a narrow band of prices for over six years until the Pool was overwhelmed by demand in 1968. Clearly the London Gold Pool was involved in the manipulation of gold prices.

The current gold "fix" in London is also a managed price based on agreement between various participants.

Dimitri Speck and many others have researched the daily price changes in gold over many years and have concluded that prices are manipulated. His analysis clearly shows the influence of the London PM fixing and the 10:00 am New York trading. An Internet search will produce graphs and considerable information on the managed and somewhat artificial gold prices.

Where one might expect random price variations, instead one sees a persistent pattern. In a world where such manipulations are both possible and largely approved of by official sources, and whereby huge profits can be generated, we should not be surprised that such manipulation exists.

Based on research it seems clear that certain times during the day strongly favor price collapses and other times favor increases. This demonstrates the influence of high frequency trading and other practices that nudge prices higher or lower to maximize profits for a small group of traders.

Another way to view gold prices is demonstrated by Nick Laird at www. sharelynx.com. He separates gold prices on the London exchange, the LBMA, into two groups. The first group calculates the results from buying gold on the AM fix and selling it on the PM fix. The second group calculates the results from buying on the PM fix and selling on the AM fix. Holding gold during the London trading hours generated substantial losses, while doing the opposite was exceptionally profitable. It seems clear these unbalanced results show a manipulated market. Given the revelations regarding manipulation of the LIBOR, crude, and other markets, the manipulation of the gold market should not be surprising.

GATA (Gold Anti-Trust Action Committee) has documented numerous examples of official government and central bank practices that manipulate gold prices.

Frankly, given the influence of leveraged futures contracts, high frequency trading, and the importance of gold, it seems nearly impossible to conceive that gold prices, along with interest rates and the stock market, are not manipulated.

The important questions are: "Since it is clear gold prices are manipulated, how can I trust gold prices, and why buy in a rigged market?"

One can dogmatically state that gold prices are manipulated and therefore any model that does not account for such manipulation cannot be accurate or valuable. Further, if the prices are manipulated, should we avoid those markets? Unfortunately, interest rates, gold, silver, stocks, options, and many other markets are manipulated to one degree or another. If we choose not to invest in manipulated markets, we will have very few choices.

Is that manipulation relevant or important over a multi-year period?

I believe that such manipulation is indeed important when viewed from a daily, weekly, or even a monthly perspective. The gold crashes that occurred in April and June 2013 were suspicious. Why would an actual seller of physical metal dump a significant percentage of total global annual production on the market in a few minutes if that seller wanted to obtain the best price for their metal? Clearly there was another motivation.

I think it has been adequately discussed and confirmed elsewhere that a huge number of naked short contracts were sold on the COMEX to suppress the COMEX price of gold. The paper contracts were sold without actual metal behind them, assuming the onslaught of so much paper gold would crash the market and allow the market manipulators to repurchase the paper contracts at a lower price and thereby book substantial profits. Manipulation obviously worked in this and many other cases. Hence we should expect it to continue as long as leveraged paper contracts are the primary mechanism for price setting in the gold market.

But has anything changed in a multi-year perspective?

Ted Butler has studied and documented the price fixing aspect of the silver and gold markets via the concentration of futures contracts and short sales over many decades. In many articles posted on the internet, he concluded on March 5, 2014 that very little had changed in the manipulation of silver and gold prices. He sees the concentrated short sellers, such as JP Morgan, who control a significant percentage of silver and gold open interest, as the manipulators.

The concentration of futures contracts, short sales, gold leasing, gold swaps, engineered market crashes and "melt-ups" in the gold and silver markets have been important and relevant to short-term prices for several decades. In spite of the gold market being managed or outright manipulated, I see only three likely interpretations regarding manipulation and the Gold Empirical Model.

a) Manipulation was either absent or unimportant during the past 42 years in the gold market. I consider this unlikely.

b) The manipulation was relevant in the short term but absorbed within the regular market volatility as the price of gold was smoothed over several years. I favor this perspective.

c) The manipulation was so overwhelming, both short-term and long-term, that it materially changed the smoothed prices for gold so much that the model variables were affected. For example, perhaps the gold prices should have been much higher subsequent to 1995 and consequently the exponents for the national debt and crude oil variables should have been larger. I cannot dismiss this perspective.

See Notes at the end of the book for more information on manipulation of the gold prices.

CHAPTER 9

IS $10,000 GOLD POSSIBLE? WHAT WOULD BE NECESSARY?

Ten thousand dollars is a nice round number. Such a price for gold might seem nearly impossible given that gold has yet to rise above $2,000 and is currently selling for about $1,300 per ounce. But in 1971 gold was selling for about $42 and rose to over $850 in less than a decade, up by more than a factor of 20.

However, we need not speculate since I have a model that projects the price of gold. What combination of national debt, crude oil, and the S&P 500 Index would be needed to generate an equilibrium gold price of $7,500, which given the volatility in the gold market, could produce a market spike to $10,000 per ounce?

National debt is currently over $17 Trillion. Assume 12% annual increases. In 9 years it could be over $50 Trillion. If we assume only 11% annual increases it would take about 10 years for the national debt to exceed $50 Trillion.

Crude oil is currently selling for about $100. Assume 12% annual increases. In 9 years it could be selling for about $300.

S&P 500 Index: Federal Reserve liquidity injections seem likely to support the stock market but wars, inflation, higher commodity prices, and government interference could significantly reduce already high P/E ratios. Assume the S&P remains more or less constant for the next several years.

Plug those values into the model and the result for the equilibrium gold price is approximately $7,500.

My conclusion is that, given our volatile and unstable world based on exponentially increasing debt and crude oil prices, $10,000 gold is a reasonable possibility. Of course policies could change, laws could be passed, peace could be favored instead of war, and the future is difficult to predict. Nevertheless, do not dismiss $10,000 gold as impossible.

It might even be a low estimate if government expenses rapidly increase due to another war, "money printing" accelerates, confidence in the US dollar erodes, and the dollar loses its reserve currency status. Like so many unbacked currencies before it, the US dollar could hyperinflate and cause unbelievable human trauma in the process. I sincerely hope that future US monetary and fiscal policies will not encourage hyperinflation.

CHAPTER 10

GOLD MARKET CYCLES

(Portions of this were originally published by the author, GE Christenson, at www.deviantinvestor.com on March 11, 2014.)

Instead of listening to self-serving opinions from bankers and biased experts, let's examine the historical data. The following chart shows monthly prices for gold since 1997. Note that highs and lows as listed in the monthly data are slightly different from actual hourly highs and lows. For this analysis over 14 years, the differences are immaterial.

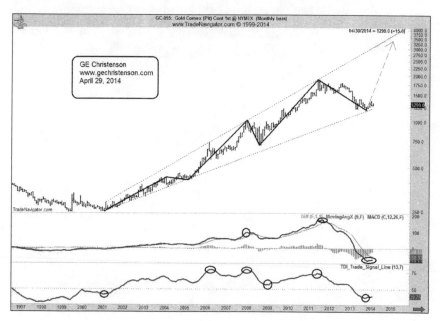

This table shows the price and approximate number of years.

Date	Low	High	Low to High (years)	High to Low (years)	Low to Low (years)	High to High (years)
Apr. 2001	$256					
Apr. 2004		$433	3.0			
May 2005	$413			1.1	4.1	
Mar. 2008		$1017	2.8			3.9
Oct. 2008	$698			0.6	3.4	
Aug. 2011		$1890	2.8			3.4
Dec. 2013	$1194			2.4	5.2	

Summary: The price of gold bottomed in 2001, rallied for 3.0 years, fell for 1.1 years, rallied for 2.8 years, fell for 0.6 years, rallied for 2.8 years, and fell for 2.4 years. **Lows were about 4 years apart, highs were about 3.5 years apart, and the rallies lasted, on average, about 3 years.**

Gold in December of 2013 had dropped to the lower logarithmic trend line after falling for 2.4 years. The patterns suggest that the next move should be a rally that lasts approximately 3 years from December 2013. It should reach new highs near the top of the trend channel well above $3,500.

Technical Analysis:

1) Gold prices made a double-bottom in December 2013 thereby indicating a successful test of the lows formed in June of 2013.
2) The MACD, a technical indicator shown in the first chart, which tracks the difference between two moving averages, registered a very low reading in December 2013. Further, the moving averages

in the indicator have turned up. This is strongly supportive of the analysis that December marked a major low in gold prices.

3) The TDI-Trade-Signal line, another technical indicator shown in the first chart, registered its lowest reading in 15 years at the June 2013 low and has also turned up. This is another strong indication that gold bottomed in December.

4) The RSI, or Relative Strength Index – a timing indicator, as shown on the second chart, was at a 15 year low at the June 2013 gold price lows. It has turned upward.

5) The disparity index, which is simply the deviation between the monthly prices and the 12 month simple moving average, as shown in the second chart, was at a 30 year low and flashing a buy signal after the June 2013 gold price lows.

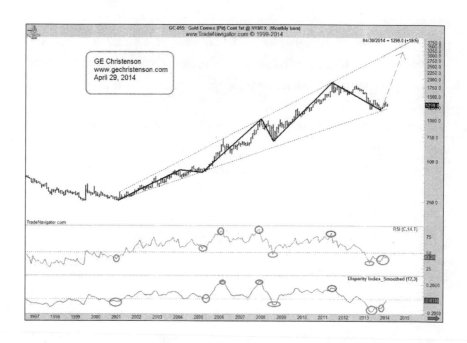

The Gold Empirical Model:

The model projects a "fair" or equilibrium price for gold in March 2014 of approximately $1,580, considerably higher than the March market price of about $1,350. Gold prices, based on this long-term model, are currently low and the next cycle should produce a move higher during 2014 - 2016.

REMEMBER:

> **During this long term bull market that started in 2001, gold should be used for saving and investing. Gold ownership buys financial security, insurance against currency devaluation, and peace of mind. This model is not designed nor intended for short term trading.**

See Notes at the end for additional gold analysis via the golden ratio and for delta timing zones.

CHAPTER 11

GOLD RATIOS TO THE DOW, SILVER, AND CRUDE OIL

DOW TO GOLD RATIO:

This ratio shows the relative value of stocks, as measured by the Dow Index, versus the price of gold. When the ratio is high, such as in the year 2000, stocks are strong and gold is weak. When the ratio is low, such as near 1:1, gold is strong and stocks are weak.

Importantly, this ratio seems to move in long term cycles and appears to be trending downward to perhaps repeat the 1:1 ratio. Such a ratio could occur at a stock market crash along with a strong demand for hard assets such as gold. For example, the Dow might drop back to 10,000 and gold might spike upward to a high of $10,000.

The current ratio as of March 2014 is about 12:1.

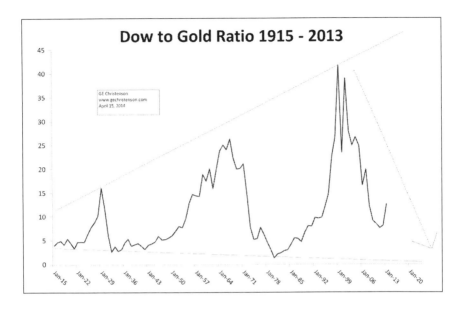

GOLD TO SILVER RATIO:

The gold to silver ratio shows the relative strength of gold versus silver. Throughout history the ratio has varied widely but a typical ratio was 10 or 20 to one. An often quoted historical ratio is 16:1.

Since the dollar has been unbacked by gold since 1971, the ratio has fluctuated wildly, from a low of about 17 to over 100.

Silver has the more volatile price, so when both gold and silver are rising, silver is typically rising more rapidly and consequently the gold to silver ratio is declining. Similarly, when the metals are weak, such as from 1980 to 2001, the ratio increases since silver falls more rapidly than gold.

The ratio is important because it shows, in broad terms, where the two metals are in their cycle from low to high to low prices. At gold and silver market tops, the ratio will be low and at bottoms the ratio will be high.

As of April 2014 the ratio is approximately 66:1. In my interpretation this is a relatively high ratio and indicates that both silver and gold have considerable room to move higher.

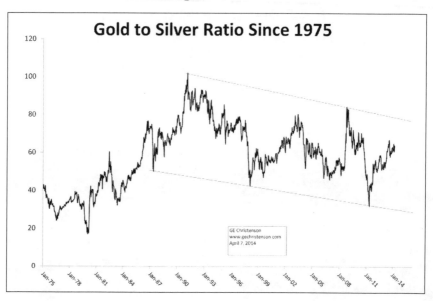

GOLD TO CRUDE RATIO:

Crude oil is the most important commodity in the world. Gold is the ultimate money but it also trades somewhat like a commodity. Examine the graph of the number of barrels that an ounce of gold will purchase.

As of March 2014 the ratio is about 13.5 – gold is priced at about 13.5 times the price of a barrel of crude oil. The average over the past 42 years has been about 15.2. Gold prices are currently low compared to the price of crude oil.

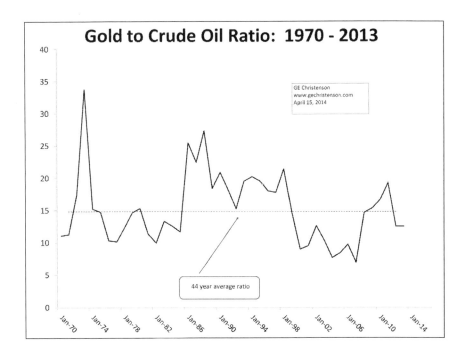

CHAPTER 12

GOLD – THE BIG PICTURE

While I consider it unlikely, the model could drastically overestimate or underestimate the price of gold in the next decade. Further, an economic collapse or new legislation might suppress the price of gold or create a new gold-backed currency in order to restore confidence in the currency. Of course a "moonshot" in the price of gold is not impossible either. There were many hyperinflations in the 20th century that should remind us that both central banks and governments have the capacity, and sometimes the willingness, to destroy the value of their currencies. The average American probably believes hyperinflation is unlikely but history has shown that it is indeed possible.

Gold has been a store of value for the past 5,000 years and is likely to be a store of value in the future, regardless of what the politicians and central bankers wish. I suspect that even if gold is declared illegal to own, it will have a substantial black market value. I think we can safely assume that gold will retain its value, on average, during the upcoming years.

If the economy collapses, as some people believe is possible, and most dismiss as craziness, the consequences might be devastating and unpredictable.

As they say, you cannot eat gold. It could be more important to own farmland that grows food. But a farmer with excess food might be happy to exchange food for gold, knowing that gold will always be accepted as money, and will be exchangeable for other items the farmer needs.

Paper dollars, or whatever is the official currency, might be shunned as nearly worthless.

Gresham's Law states that bad money will drive out good money. If the purchasing value of the dollar plummets, then people will hoard gold and silver, as they will be perceived as good money. History has recorded hundreds of examples of paper money losing its value while gold and silver have retained their value when measured in the commodities we need for daily life.

People living in the United States have little experience with hyperinflations but the people of South America and Europe have clear memories of the value of paper money evaporating. An example is Argentina – they have devalued their currency by removing eight zeroes over the past 30 plus years. Rampant inflation is the norm, not the exception, when irresponsible governments issue unbacked paper currency. Gold protects purchasing power from such currency devaluations.

Gold may not reach $10,000 any time soon, but it is far more likely to increase in price and retain its purchasing power than digital dollars deposited in a saving account or Certificate of Deposit yielding a percent or less.

Think ahead to the year 2021. Would you rather have 100 ounces of gold in 2021, about $135,000 in today's dollars, or a saving account that grew from $135,000 to $160,000 between now and the year 2021? I believe that 100 ounces of gold will be much more valuable and that few people currently understand this concept. Further, I expect that by 2021 most people will realize that 100 ounces of gold will purchase far more food, energy, and housing than $160,000, or perhaps even $500,000.

We all make choices regarding our savings and investments. Consider gold coins and bars to preserve your purchasing power, protect against counter-party risk, and compensate for the certain devaluation of dollars, euros, and yen.

PART 2

MORE REASONS TO OWN GOLD

Part 1 discussed gold as a store of value, inflation of the money supply, and that my model projects gold prices will rise considerably higher, such as to $5,000 - $10,000 within the next decade.

Part 2 addresses:

- Counter-party risk
- The Fed, interest rates, QE, and inflation
- Central bank gold sales

REMEMBER:

> **During this long term bull market that started in 2001, gold should be used for saving and investing. Gold ownership buys financial security, insurance against currency devaluation, and peace of mind. This model is not designed nor intended for short term trading.**

CHAPTER 13

COUNTER-PARTY RISK

A simple example may help explain counter-party risk and why it will become an important concern in the event of another financial crash.

Suppose a financial institution, such as Lehman Brothers, is insolvent. Many other institutions own derivative contracts backed by Lehman, the counter-party. But since Lehman is insolvent, those other institutions probably will not get paid when they try to collect on their derivative contracts. Positions that, pre-crisis, were believed to be fully hedged, could quickly become unhedged "naked" positions with the full nominal value of the derivative contract at risk. The risk to the over-leveraged Too-Big-To-Fail banks could change from manageable to overwhelming in short order. This could happen in New York, London, Germany, or elsewhere. It hardly matters where the initial spark actually occurs when the global financial system is, figuratively speaking, kindling ready to burst into flame. Further, the monetary systems are interconnected so deeply that a large failure in one spot could damage the entire system.

Due to the size and quantity of those derivative obligations, the failure to pay on those derivative contracts would render many more financial institutions insolvent. And those institutions would be unable to pay their derivative obligations to other institutions, and that explains how the daisy-chain of failed derivative contracts would expand.

In such a scenario banks do not trust each other, institutions are uncertain if they will be paid, or if they can pay their obligations, and confidence in the system is destroyed. This is, more or less, what happened in 2008.

It could happen again. The next financial crisis, when it occurs, might be far worse. It appears that the too-big-to-fail banks have become even larger since 2008, more leveraged, more risky, and more subject to systemic failure. The monetary system is global, interconnected and interdependent. While small failures can probably be absorbed and managed, larger failures could collapse the entire system as critically important trust and confidence evaporate. Unfortunately, the added leverage provided by the use of derivatives increases the instability of the system and thereby magnifies the risk of another meltdown. As long as the monetary system is functional and confidence in the system remains, derivatives generate large profits for the banks and those profits ensure their continued use. But as 2008 has shown us, minor perturbations can develop into massive failures given the leverage, risk and potential instabilities in the global monetary system.

Perhaps the Fed will create enough dollars to keep the bubbles inflated, or perhaps not. If the Fed is called upon to bail out all Too-Big-To-Fail banks the Fed could spark hyperinflationary fears and destroy confidence in currencies, particularly the US dollar. Alternatively the Fed may have reached the limit of their practical capacity to create dollars and, in a monetary crisis, the world might be forced to seek support from the International Monetary Fund (IMF) or return to some form of gold standard. Another crisis could necessitate restructuring of our current monetary system, damage the reserve currency status of the dollar, cause a default on much of the $100 Trillion in global debt, and hopefully regulate and reduce the use of derivative contracts. The price of gold could jump, in a relatively short time, to multiples of its current price. Similarly the prices for food and energy would rise sufficiently to create social protests, riots, and bloodshed. The short-term consequences will not be pretty.

In any case, counter-party risk is important when considering any debt-based financial product. Those products are promises to pay and are only as good as the institution and collateral that backs those promises. This includes:

- T-Bonds
- T-Notes
- Gold futures contracts
- Oil futures contracts
- Dollars, which are debt based Federal Reserve Notes and a liability of the Federal Reserve
- Brokerage accounts
- Bank deposits, legally defined as liabilities of the bank and not your money
- Mortgages
- Some pension plans
- Many more

Examples of counter-party risk – very simplified:

You own a 10 year T-note from the government of Spain. The counter-party is the government of Spain. Will the government repay the loan or default?

You own 1,000 shares of stock in IBM through your broker. The broker has hypothecated your shares for trading purposes and has looted customer accounts to meet margin calls. This is essentially what happened with MFGlobal when over $1Billion in customer money went "missing." You could have counter-party risk with your broker.

You own 2,000 shares of stock in IBM through your broker. The broker clears transactions through a clearing house which has quietly become insolvent. The clearing house owes your broker and while you and your broker are solvent, you may still be at risk due to the insolvency of the clearing house. It is likely that you have more counter-party risk that you believe.

You have $1,000,000 in dollars deposited in various Certificates of Deposit at several banks. The world financial powers, at some future time, dethrone the US dollar as the world's reserve currency. Another currency, the Special Drawing Rights of the IMF, or a basket of currencies, is chosen for international payments. In that case foreign governments no longer need to hold as many dollars so those excess dollars come flooding back to the United States to purchase buildings, materials, land, gold and anything but Treasury bonds and other debt paper. The Federal Reserve tries to support the dollar but is overwhelmed by the sheer volume of returning dollars. The value of the dollar rapidly drops by 25% or more in terms of commodity prices, such as crude oil, wheat, and gold, and consequently your $1,000,000 has been reduced in purchasing power by at least 25%. Since all those dollars are Federal Reserve Notes or liabilities of the Federal Reserve, you have counter-party risk with the Federal Reserve.

You have $2,000,000 deposited at a major bank, one known as a "Too-Big-To-Fail" bank, which has derivatives risk of approximately $100 Trillion dollars while it has capital of approximately $1 Trillion. A financial crisis occurs, the counter-parties to many of those derivative contracts demand payment from your bank, and the bank is unable to pay all its obligations. Replicating what was done in Cyprus in 2013, the bank determines that "bail-ins" are needed, and converts $500,000 of your deposited funds into restricted stock in the insolvent, and possibly bankrupt, bank. Perhaps the $500,000 is gone forever or perhaps a portion will eventually be returned.

As of this writing in March 2014 it appears that currency wars and financial wars are accelerating. The United States and Russia need not lob bombs at each other when they can unleash viruses, sanctions, hackers, and derivatives upon the other combatant in order to damage economies, bank solvency, and currency values. In a world where cyber-space is increasingly real and important, an attack upon a network, an exchange, a banking system, or other financial systems could be devastating. The counter-party risk of digital accounts will increase when countries engage in financial and currency wars. Not only can fiat currencies be devalued, but the accounts where those currencies are stored can be hacked and the currencies stolen more easily. As John Rubino says, *"the proper response to peak complexity is hyper-simplification via gold, silver and farmland."*

It is critical to note that gold and silver bullion have NO COUNTER-PARTY RISK. They are assets without an obligation to or from any other asset, debt, government, or financial institution.

Repeat: Physical gold and silver have no counter-party risk, unlike almost all other non-tangible assets. In the event of a monetary or economic collapse, possession of physical gold and silver will be important to your financial survival and perhaps your life. However, in a monetary collapse gold and silver may be practically unavailable to buy, regardless of price. There is no fever like "gold fever" and desperate people will go to great lengths to convert their evaporating financial assets into physical gold. But in such a collapse, those who own physical gold may be unwilling to sell their gold in exchange for more paper promises from governments and central banks.

A currency collapse or a monetary collapse is far removed from the consciousness of a majority of citizens in the western world, especially in the United States. A typical response might be *"that could never happen,"* because it has not happened in recent memory and it conjures images of a "Mad Max" post-apocalyptic world. In fact, such a collapse is quite possible. The world has experienced several global monetary system collapses in the past, such as in 1914, 1939, and 1971. All were related to a collapse in confidence in currencies, banks, economies and governments.

Note that the first two were followed by world wars and the third was partially induced by the expenses of the Vietnam War. The world moved on, paper currencies were devalued, some people lost the majority of their savings and pensions, and the world reformed the monetary system to facilitate trade and global financial transactions. Those individuals who kept their savings in gold survived all such collapses far better than those who trusted paper promises.

At this time it seems likely that a collapse in confidence in the value of at least one of the yen, the euro, or the dollar is practically inevitable. Perhaps the yen will be the first victim, perhaps the devaluation will be a slow-motion collapse, or perhaps the collapse will occur in the space of a few weeks. The world financial systems are non-linear and such systems are subject to small stimuli which can cause massive and rapid changes when those systems react at a point of instability. As the big banks become larger, as they increase their leverage, as they sell more derivative contracts, and as governments increase their debt loads, the financial world becomes increasingly unstable, more vulnerable to a crisis in confidence, and subject to a rapid and destructive response to "black swans." Counter-party risk appears to be very high and increasing. It has been clearly demonstrated that most people and institutions cannot "get out in time" and that the financial exits are narrow and overloaded in a time of crisis and panic.

Avoid the counter-party risk and the potential panic resulting from another monetary collapse, and convert some of your assets into physical gold, preferably stored in a vault outside the country of your residence.

See Notes at the end for more discussion on counter-party risk.

CHAPTER 14

THE FED, INTEREST RATES, QE, AND INFLATION

There are other reasons to own gold and to act upon the projections of the Gold Empirical Model:

Through their immense control over the money supply and interest rates, the Federal Reserve has implemented such programs as ZIRP - Zero Interest Rate Program, QE - Quantitative Easing, and Operation Twist, which lowered long term interest rates to generational lows. If the Federal Reserve cannot maintain generational low interest rates forever, the interest expense on that incredibly large mountain of debt will eventually become overwhelming.

The current (March 2014) official national debt is approximately $17.5 Trillion. Interest expense on that debt is quite low since the yield on short term debt is nearly zero and even 30 year T-Bonds yield less than 4%. The official national debt is increasing exponentially and will soon reach $20 Trillion and eventually $30 Trillion.

Assume that the average interest rate paid by the US government when the national debt reaches $30 Trillion is 6%. The annual interest expense will then be about $1.8 Trillion. For perspective, the entire revenue of the US government for 2014 will be approximately $3 Trillion. It seems inevitable that the Federal Reserve will create enough new dollars to pay the interest expense and roll over the maturing debts rather than default. Eventually the consequences of present and future "money printing" will work their way into the real economy and create consumer price inflation, especially in the commodities that we need for daily living.

The interest expense will become a larger problem as the runaway debt mountain continues to grow. It is not difficult to imagine that exponentially increasing debt will eventually end in a crash – a deflationary depression, an inflationary depression, or a combination of inflation in some assets and deflation in other assets. It seems likely that hard assets, such as gold, silver, land, and diamonds, will inflate in price while paper assets will, relatively speaking, deflate in price. Of course the political and financial elite wish to keep the currency and debt bubbles inflated as long as possible so expect even more extreme overvaluations and subsequent crashes in those markets.

The Fed, the IMF, and other central banks, have openly stated that they are working to create inflation and that deflation is to be avoided at all costs. They will do "whatever it takes" to create their desired inflation. "Whatever it takes" has included many $Trillions in created currency, more $Trillions in swaps and guarantees, and other extraordinary measures to fight deflation and create inflation. If the Fed and other central banks initially fail in their efforts to avoid deflation we should expect even more radical responses, including, as a last resort, an upward revaluation in the price of gold. If they succeed in creating inflation via their various money-printing schemes, the price of gold and the cost of consumer goods will certainly rise as people realize that the value of currencies is declining. We should expect that central banks will, one way or another, force the price of gold much higher as a consequence of their fiat currency policies and the overwhelming weight of global debt. As the global reserve currency, the dollar has perhaps the most to lose and the farthest to fall.

Historically speaking, once governments and central banks decide to issue unbacked debt based paper and digital currencies and continually spend in excess of their revenues, they eventually accelerate the creation of their currencies and their debasement. The result is a massive inflation in consumer prices.

Central banking was initiated about three centuries ago in England. At that time the "pound sterling" was supposedly backed by one pound of silver. After three centuries of inflation, one paper British pound now purchases less than 1/10 of an ounce of silver.

The Federal Reserve was created in 1913 when gold was priced under $21 per ounce. Today, after 100 years of "money printing" and inflation, gold is priced at about $1,350 per ounce. Viewed from a different perspective, the value of the US dollar has declined by about 98% in the past 100 years, and the majority of that purchasing power has been lost since 1971 when the gold backing for the dollar was eliminated by President Nixon.

History has clearly shown that paper money does not hold its value. Voltaire (1694-1778) remarked, almost 300 years ago, *"Paper money eventually returns to its intrinsic value – zero."* The declining purchasing power of the dollar since 1971 has shown that Voltaire's observation is still accurate. As the dollar inevitably declines in value, perhaps sooner rather than later, the price of gold will increase. Depending on the degree of devaluation, a gold price of $5,000 - $10,000 might be much too low. Unthinkable? The citizens of Argentina, Zimbabwe, and many other countries will assure us that hyperinflation and the destruction of their currency's purchasing power are quite possible.

How many paper British pounds, euros or dollars will be needed to purchase one ounce of gold in another 10 or 20 years? The answer might be shocking.

See Notes at the end for a partial list of hyper inflated currencies.

CHAPTER 15

CENTRAL BANK GOLD SALES

The official gold holdings in central banks have been widely discussed and published. The top four official holdings, per Wikipedia, are:

The United States	8,133 tons
Germany	3,390 tons
IMF	2,814 tons
Italy	2,451 tons

I see a number of concerns with these official statements. A few are:

- Central banks "lease" gold to bullion banks, which sell the gold into the market. However, even though the gold has been sold and is no longer in the central bank vaults, it still is considered a central bank asset.
- Central banks are not transparent regarding their gold holdings. Secrecy is the norm. Many have suggested that obfuscation and partial truths are also standard procedure.
- Central bankers have admitted on several occasions that they manage gold prices, lease gold, sell gold, and swap gold to promote stability in their paper currencies and to limit the rise in gold prices.
- There has been no audit of the United States gold in over 50 years. There is much speculation as to the amount of gold, if any, that remains, unencumbered, and physically in the vaults.

- In 2013 Germany requested the return of 300 tons of German owned gold, out of a total of over 1,500 tons officially stored at the New York Fed. That gold was not returned. The NY Fed stated that it would take seven years to return the 300 tons. During the first year, it has been reported that only five tons of gold were actually returned to Germany. Perhaps this was merely a distraction and a response to some political need, or perhaps it was simple recognition of the fact that it is difficult to return gold which has previously been "leased" or sold and is no longer stored in the vault.

- China reports their official gold holdings only when they wish to do so. The last report was over 5 years ago. Since then gold imports into China from Hong Kong, Switzerland, London, New York and other locations have accelerated to the point of speculation that:

  a) The imports into China have been so large that the only possible sources seem to have been western central banks.

  b) Swiss refineries have accepted huge quantities of gold from the United States, England, and other western countries, refined it to 99.99% kilo bars and shipped those bars to China.

  c) It has been calculated by Alasdair Macleod of Goldmoney that the increase in total private plus Chinese central bank holdings since 2008 could be in excess of 10,000 tons. China continues to import gold from the western world and does not export gold. China is the largest gold mining country in the world and has a strong cultural affinity for gold and hard assets. The Chinese value gold over paper, which is clear from their private and official acquisition of a huge quantity of gold in the past six years.

  d) It has been suggested that most of the United States gold is gone, leased, sold, or otherwise missing.

Actual accounting, hard data, and answers may be forthcoming in the future, but at this time, the above is intelligent speculation.

What is important is that since Central Banks have been selling gold into the market, they have temporarily increased the supply of gold and thereby kept the price lower than it might otherwise have been. However, this begs the question, what happens when there is no more gold that western central banks are able or willing to sell or lease? There are a number of articles listed in the notes which suggest that much of the gold previously held in London and the United States has been removed from those vaults, per official export data, and shipped to Switzerland for melting and casting into the 99.99% kilo bars favored in Asia.

If the supply of this central bank gold diminishes and the demand from Asia remains strong, there is little doubt that the price for gold must rise substantially. I know of no way to estimate future prices based on supply and demand data, but my model projects much higher gold prices in the future based on other macro-economic numbers, and one large driver of those higher prices could be decreased supply of gold confronted by the continuing large demand from Asia.

If the western central banks are selling gold to suppress its price and to support their paper currencies, and if the Chinese and Russians are purchasing that gold to hedge against a falling dollar, it is temporarily in the best interests of both the Western and Asian countries to keep the price low. Of course gold prices will automatically adjust higher when the artificial supply from the western central bank vaults is inevitably diminished or terminated.

See Notes at the end for information and additional analysis on central bank gold sales, gold price manipulation and suppression.

PART 3

ACTION PLANS

Part 1 demonstrated the need for an empirical model that calculates gold prices based on macro-economic variables. My model projects substantially higher gold prices, perhaps $5,000 to $10,000 in the next decade.

Part 2 discussed counter-party risk, Quantitative Easing, consumer price inflation, gold that central banks supposedly hold in their vaults, and how these indicate we must own gold as insurance against the ongoing destruction of the world's unbacked fiat currencies.

Part 3 offers suggestions on how to purchase gold, where to purchase and store gold, when to sell, and what a bubble in the gold market could indicate for prices.

CHAPTER 16

HOW AND WHERE TO PURCHASE GOLD

Much has been written on how to purchase and store gold. The following is a simple and quick summary to assist in your decision making process. I encourage you to consult with a professional who understands the gold market. I have listed a number of reputable American and European dealers in the notes at the end of the book.

Begin by defining your needs, goals, timeline, and resources.

- Do you want to trade gold in the short term?
- Are you a long term investor who intends to hold gold for many years, perhaps never selling, and willing it to your heirs?
- Do you love old coins or are bars acceptable?
- Do you wish to have your coins and bars in your possession?
- Do you have a properly hidden and safe storage location?
- Do you want to pay a professional storage company to store your coins and bars in a secure and insured vault?
- Do you want your coins and bars in the same country as your residence, or do you want your gold stored in another country such as Switzerland or Singapore?
- Are your funds available in a tax-sheltered plan such as an IRA or are they after tax funds? You can purchase physical gold in an IRA!

If you have considered these questions and are clear as to your resources and your needs, you are ready to make specific choices.

Short Term Trading:

- The easiest are Exchange Traded Funds - ETFs. The most popular is the SPDR Gold Shares fund, symbol GLD. I recommend the iShares Gold Trust, symbol IAU, Central Gold Trust, symbol GTU, and Sprott Physical Gold Trust, symbol PHYS. In the event of a monetary crisis, there is some risk associated with all ETFs. I encourage you to investigate them carefully.
- Another option is the Canadian closed-end mutual fund Central Fund of Canada, symbol CEF. It invests in physical gold and silver and stores both in vaults in Canada. It is readily tradable in your brokerage account but you can also invest in CEF for the long term.
- Futures contracts with minimal margin can be highly profitable but are always dangerous, especially in manipulated markets. Trading gold futures is like playing Blackjack in Las Vegas against a skilled card mechanic who uses marked cards. You might win and some people do, but ETFs, coins and bars purchased with no margin are considerably safer and less stressful.

Long Term Investing:

- Coins or Bars? Coins and small bars are liquid, portable, and valuable anywhere in the world. Bars are available in many sizes, such as 10g, 1 ounce, 100g, as well as 10 ounces, 1 kilo, 100 ounces, and 400 ounces. If you plan to leave your gold in a vault for long term storage, bars are a good choice.
- Your possession or in a vault? Some people are only comfortable if their gold is physically in their possession. Others want the

safety and security of a professional vault. I encourage you to consider the safety of a professional vault outside the banking system.

- Most gold dealers will arrange for vault storage if you wish. Annual fees and transportation charges may be involved. Most professionals recommend against using a safe deposit box in a commercial bank; they prefer private insured storage outside the banking system.

- Domestic or Offshore? You may find it safer and more secure to have your gold stored offshore in a vault where there is more privacy and security than in your own country. Many gold dealers can arrange for such offshore purchase and storage.

- Counterfeit coins and bars: While fake coins exist, it is more likely that fakes will be larger bars. I have been told that a counterfeit bar will fool most people, however sophisticated non-invasive tests can easily determine authenticity. The safe approach is to purchase your coins and bars from a reputable gold dealer.

- Numismatic coins can be beautiful, historic, and profitable, if you know and understand the market. Be certain you know and trust your dealer.

- You can purchase certain gold and silver coins in your IRA account without creating a taxable transaction. You are not allowed to take delivery of the coins and they must be stored professionally. Most gold dealers can direct you to a company which will manage the paperwork, purchase, delivery, and storage of your tax-sheltered gold.

A partial list of gold dealers is shown in the notes at the end of the book. Most of those dealers can arrange for professional storage, and if desired, for storage in Switzerland, Canada, Hong Kong, and Singapore.

WHEN SHOULD YOU PURCHASE GOLD? This depends upon your needs, resources, and plans. My suggestions include:

1) Purchase whenever the market price is less than the equilibrium or fair value as calculated by my model. As of March 2014 the calculated fair value is about $1,580 or about 1,145 euros. Prices below $1,580 seem very likely to produce long term profits.

2) Avoid or reduce your purchases when the market price is well above the equilibrium or fair value. The most recent example was August of 2011 when market prices exceeded the equilibrium price by about 30%.

3) Many people find that a dollar-cost-average system is useful in their long term buying strategy. Purchase a fixed dollar amount of gold every month or quarter and thereby assure yourself of buying more ounces at lower prices. Some purchases will be made at prices which subsequently appear too high but in the current gold bull market they will eventually become profitable.

4) **An improved variation on the dollar-cost-averaging system is to adjust your dollar purchases up or down depending on the percentage the market price is below or above the equilibrium price. Example: when the market price is 20% below the equilibrium price, buy 40% more than usual. When the market price is 20% above the equilibrium price, buy 40% less than usual.**

5) Purchase whenever you can comfortably exchange paper dollars or euros for real physical gold. In 10 years I expect you will look back upon this choice as an excellent exchange.

CHAPTER 17

WHEN TO SELL GOLD

(Portions of this were originally published by the author, GE Christenson, at www.deviantinvestor.com on December 6, 2012.)

What is your intention?

a) Hold your gold because you want to own it for the rest of your life and pass it on to your grandchildren.

   or

b) Sell your gold now, which is a big mistake in my opinion, because you believe that gold is in a bubble, downtrend, or never should have been bought.

Most of us will sell sometime between now and never. What is an objective method to determine when to sell?

Technical ratios which suggest it might be sensible to sell some of your gold:

- Sell some gold when the gold to silver ratio drops below 20 to 1. The gold to silver ratio is currently (April 2014) about 66 to 1. When gold and silver prices have both risen beyond all typical expectations, the ratio will probably drop to between 10 and 20 to 1. The ratio was about 17 to 1 at the bubble peak in 1980, which was a good time to sell.

- Sell some gold when the Dow Jones Industrial Average (Dow) ratio to gold (Dow/Gold) has dropped to near 1 to 1. The ratio is currently about 12 to 1. The ratio could reach 2 to 1, for example, if the Dow was priced at 20,000 and gold was selling for $10,000 per ounce. At the peak of the 1980 gold bubble the ratio was approximately 1 to 1.
- Sell some gold when the gold to crude oil ratio rises to perhaps 25 to 1. For example if crude oil is priced at $300 per barrel and gold is priced at $7,500, that is a 25 to 1 ratio.
- Sell some gold when you can pay the outstanding mortgage on your house with a small amount of gold, perhaps 10 to 20 ounces. Of course this may not be necessary or make sense in your individual circumstances, but it could be an excellent choice in the event of a huge price increase in gold without a reset in debt levels.
- I suggest you sell only some of your gold because it is always sensible to keep some "real money" and not be utterly dependent upon unbacked paper currency which includes many counter-party risks.

Sentiment-based timing to consider selling gold:

- Sell some gold when the "money honeys" on financial TV are running a story every hour on the rapidly rising price of gold.
- Sell some gold when Time magazine posts a picture of gold bars on their cover with a caption such as, "The Unstoppable Bull Market in Gold."
- Sell some gold when your hairdresser/barber gushes about the gold s/he just bought and how it is certain to triple in price soon.
- Sell some gold when there are long lines of people waiting at coin shops to buy gold.
- Sell some gold when people finally realize that unbacked paper currencies are accepted only because others will accept the currency, and people are losing confidence in the currency.

Jim Sinclair suggests that, regarding gold, people should "buy fish lines and sell rhino horns." Stated another way, when the price has collapsed in a spike down (looks like a line extending downward from a fishing pole) then we should buy. But if the price has risen in a parabolic pattern (looks like a rhino horn), then it is time to sell a portion and wait for the correction.

If the price has fallen too far, too fast, and there is no fundamental reason for the price collapse, buy more. If the price has rapidly rallied to new highs far beyond expectations, then it has moved too far, too fast. Those crazy markets rallies, whether in gold, silver, the NASDAQ 100, crude oil, or real estate, always correct in a crash. Examples include gold and silver in early 1980, the Nikkei 225 in 1990, and the NASDAQ 100 in early 2000.

It seems likely that gold and silver will accelerate into a parabolic rise within a few years unless the central bank money printing ceases. However, I believe we should expect the money printing and bond monetization, in one form or another, to continue for a long time.

The common denominators in such a scenario are the human emotions of fear and greed. Greed drives the market to new highs and fear causes the crash. People were "getting rich quick" when the NASDAQ 100 rallied from about 1,100 to about 5,000 in less than two years when greed was dominant. But when the NASDAQ 100 reached a natural stopping point, fear took over and people sold in panic or to preserve what value remained. If they did not sell, and rode the market all the way down, they lost a significant portion of their investment and paper profits. Fear motivated people to sell, which created more fear and selling, and the waterfall decline fed upon itself until the sellers were exhausted.

Similarly, in 2008, when gold had collapsed from over $1,000 to under $700 (the price as of March 2014 is about $1,350) in seven months, most amateur investors were reluctant to buy because they were fearful that the price of gold would decline further. Professionals buy the bottoms and sell the tops. Fearful amateurs sell down into the bottoms and then buy back near the tops when greed is overwhelming.

If you bought gold, which is currently in a long term uptrend, then waiting will eventually bring success, even if you purchased at the temporary top in August 2011. However, if you were buying Enron stock some years ago, then holding a losing position only magnified the disastrous investment. Study the fundamentals and intrinsic value of your investments until you understand the differences. Gold and Enron stock are materially different investments.

The Bottom Line: Buy when the "blood is running in the streets" and sell when everyone else wants to buy. Use ratios and comparisons to other markets as objective measures to indicate probable price extremes in markets. We can seldom pick the precise bottoms and tops, but we can carefully observe and act while others are being swept along by their own fears and greed.

If we can keep our heads while others are losing theirs, and make sound decisions based on a proven model, numbers, analysis, and comparison ratios, we will make intelligent and informed buy and sell decisions. For 2014, it makes sense to hold gold and silver, and to carefully evaluate everything else. Massive and supposedly unexpected changes can occur with surprising rapidity.

The model shows that a "fair" price for gold in March of 2014 is about $1,580. Given 5,000 years of history in which gold has been a store of value, and given 42 years of recent history in which the model accurately tracked the smoothed price of gold, I feel confident in stating the following:

1) Gold is currently undervalued and likely to move higher in 2014 and 2015.
2) 42 years of history suggest that I can place reasonable trust in my model and its conclusions.
3) I think it will serve you well to convert some of your paper wealth into gold. Whether it is 10% or 90% is a decision dependent upon

your circumstances and your faith in governments, central banks, and the unbacked fiat currency system.

4) I see few fundamental or technical reasons why gold should continue its downward path much longer. However I am certain that large Too-Big-To-Fail banks have published self-serving reasons why they believe gold will continue falling.

5) I encourage you to think for yourself, read the opinions of many experts, consider the model results, and make investment decisions regarding gold that fit within your comfort zone.

CHAPTER 18

MARKET BUBBLES AND IMPLICATIONS FOR GOLD PRICES

(Portions of this were originally published by the author, GE Christenson, at www.deviantinvestor.com on January 28, 2013.)

Definitions:

- Bubble: A speculative mania in a market that is priced well beyond what the fundamentals and intrinsic value indicate.
- Phase 1: The first phase of the bubble begins with the price bottoming and initiating a long rally. It is often indicated by a triggering event such as President Nixon closing the "gold window" on August 15, 1971, the beginning of the gold and silver bubbles that peaked in 1980. The market rallies for some years, hits a new "all-time" high, and then corrects.

The market proceeds into a bubble phase when it rallies beyond that new high and continues upward. The end of phase 1 and the beginning of phase 2 are the point at which the market rallies from its correction low and exceeds its previous high. See the graph of the gold market with the indicated beginning and end points for phase 1 and phase 2.

- Phase 2: The final phase of the bubble starts when the price exceeds the "new high" and then rallies to a much higher and unsustainable level.

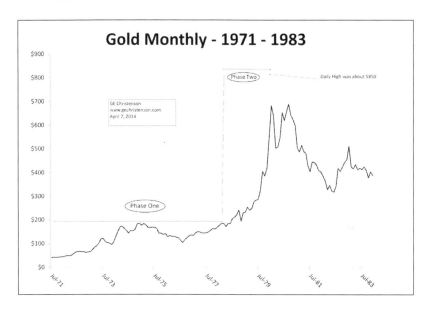

The above chart of gold from 1971 – 1983 shows the bubble in gold, the incredible price rise in phase two of the bubble, and the ensuing crash.

I looked at the time and price data for the South Sea Bubble in England from 1719 -1720, the silver bubble from August 1971 to January 1980, the NASDAQ bubble from August 1982 to March 2000, the Japanese Real Estate bubble from 1965 to 1991, the gold bubble from August 1971 to January 1980, and the S&P mini-bubble from August 1982 to March of 2000. All prices and dates are approximate as this is "big picture" analysis.

My conclusion is that bubbles start slowly and then accelerate to unsustainable highs (on large volume) that are largely created by greed and fear but not fundamental evaluations. Bubbles generally follow the "Pareto Principal" where approximately 80% of the price move occurs in the last 20% of the time. Consider:

Gold Bubble:

- Phase 1: August 1971 to July 1978. Price from $40 to $200.
- Phase 2: July 1978 to January 1980. Price from $200 to $870.
- Time: Phase 1 - 82%, phase 2 – 18%.
- Price: Phase 1 – 19%, phase 2 – 81%. Phase 2 price ratio: 4.4

Silver Bubble: (Extreme price bubble)

- Phase 1: August 1971 to October 1978. Price from $1.50 to $6.40.
- Phase 2: October 1978 to January 1980. Price from $6.40 to $50.
- Time: Phase 1 - 85%, phase 2 – 15%.
- Price: Phase 1 – 10%, phase 2 – 90%. Phase 2 price ratio: 7.8

South Sea Bubble: (Extreme price bubble)

- Phase 1: January 1719 to March 1720. Price from 120 to 180.
- Phase 2: March 1720 to July 1720. Price from 180 to 900.
- Time: Phase 1 - 75%, phase 2 – 25%.
- Price: Phase 1 – 8%, phase 2 – 92%. Phase 2 price ratio: 5

NASDAQ Bubble: (Extreme price bubble)

- Phase 1: August 1982 to February 1995. Price from 168 to 780.
- Phase 2: February 1995 to March 2000. Price from 780 to 4880.
- Time: Phase 1 - 71%, phase 2 – 29%.
- Price: Phase 1 – 13%, phase 2 – 87%. Phase 2 price ratio: 6.3

Japanese Real Estate Bubble: (approximate numbers)

- Phase 1: 1960 to 1979. Price Index from 4 to 50.
- Phase 2: 1979 to 1991. Price Index from 50 to 225.
- Time: Phase 1 - 61%, phase 2 – 39%.
- Price: Phase 1 – 21%, phase 2 – 79%. Phase 2 price ratio: 4.5

S&P 500 Index Bubble: (Mini-bubble)

- Phase 1: August 1982 to February 1995. Price from 100 to 483.
- Phase 2: February 1995 to March 2000. Price from 483 to 1574.
- Time: Phase 1 - 71%, phase 2 – 29%.
- Price: Phase 1 – 26%, phase 2 – 74%. Phase 2 price ratio: 3.3

SUMMARY:

- Bubbles tend to follow the 80/20 ratio indicated in the Pareto Principle.
- Phase 1 takes approximately 70-80% of the time and covers approximately 10-20% of the total price change.
- Phase 2 accelerates taking only 20-30% of the time but covers 80-90% of the price change.
- Extreme bubbles such as the South Sea Bubble and the Silver bubble experience approximately 90% of their price change in the 2nd phase.
- The ratio of the phase 2 ending price to beginning price is typically 4 to 8 – a huge price move. Such bubbles are rare and the subsequent crash is usually devastating.

FUTURE BUBBLES:

In the opinion of many analysts, sovereign debt is an ongoing bubble that could burst with world-wide consequences. Should deficit spending and bond monetization (Quantitative Easing or "money printing") accelerate, the sovereign debt bubble will inflate further. Because of the massive printing of dollars its value must fall, particularly against commodities such as oil, gold and silver. As the purchasing power of the dollar falls, an increasing number of people will realize their dollars are losing value and some of those people will seek safety for their savings and retirement. Gold and silver will benefit from an increasingly desperate search for safety as a consequence of the decline of the dollar. Assuming the 80/20 "rule" and the phase 2 price change ratio of approximately 5, what could happen if gold rises into another speculative bubble?

Gold began its uptrend in April 2001 at $255 and rallied to a new high of about $1900 in 2011. Assume that gold surpasses its high in late 2014 or 2015, and accelerates into phase 2 thereafter. Using these assumptions phase 1 for gold would measure about 14 years and phase 2 could last until 2017-2019. If we assume that phase 1 was a move from $255 to $1,900 and represents 20% of the total move, the high could be $8,000 - $9,000.

A NON-BUBBLE SCENARIO:

Suppose the world devolves into another monetary crisis and we discover that central banks and governments are not able to "print" their way out of the crisis. James Rickards discusses this in his book, "The Death of Money." Even though central banks and governments are likely to resist the idea, it might become necessary to revalue the price of gold to a much larger price in order to support the debt markets, restore confidence in currencies, and reestablish trust in the financial markets. In this case Mr. Rickards states that the gold price might initially be set at $7,000 to $10,000 and allowed to adjust from there.

There will be ugly consequences for most people in the western world, but the financial systems must function in order to produce and transport food, energy and other necessities. In this case the revaluation of gold might be more sudden than in a multi-month bubble rally and there might be only a minimal correction in the gold price subsequent to the stabilization of the financial markets.

Is $7,000 - $10,000 GOLD OUTRAGEOUS?

Well, yes, at first glance, those prices do seem outrageous. But consider for perspective:

a) Apple stock rose from about $4 in 1997 to over $700 in 2012.
b) Silver rose from $1.50 to $50.00 in less than 10 years.
c) Gold rose from about $40 to over $850 in less than 10 years.
d) Crude oil rose from less than $11 in 1998 to almost $150 in 2008.
e) The official US national debt is larger than $17,000,000,000,000. The unfunded liabilities, depending on who is counting, are approximately $100,000,000,000,000 to $230,000,000,000,000. Divide $200 Trillion by approximately 300,000,000 people and the unfunded debt per capita of the United States is approximately $700,000. That is outrageous!
f) The official national debt increases by about $3,000,000,000 per day, each and every day. The unfunded liabilities increase by perhaps three - ten times that amount.
g) We still pretend the national debt is not a problem and that it will be "rolled over" forever. That is both delusional and outrageous.
h) Argentina has revalued their currency several times in the last 30 years. They have dropped 8 zeroes off their currency since 1980. Savings accounts and the middle class were devastated each time. It will happen again in other countries.

Given the above for perspective, is gold at $5,000 to $10,000 per ounce unreasonable, impossible, or outrageous? Certainly not! Past bubbles have had an ending price 4 – 8 times higher than the phase 2 beginning price, so history has shown that such prices for gold are indeed possible.

CONCLUSIONS

Using only the three macro-economic variables of official US national debt, the price of crude oil, and the S&P 500 Index, I have produced a model for the price of gold that replicates, on average, the smoothed price of gold. The calculated price and the smoothed market prices for gold may not precisely and graphically match each other, but they do, on average, approximate each other well over the course of 42 years.

This graph, which was shown previously, demonstrates this correlation:

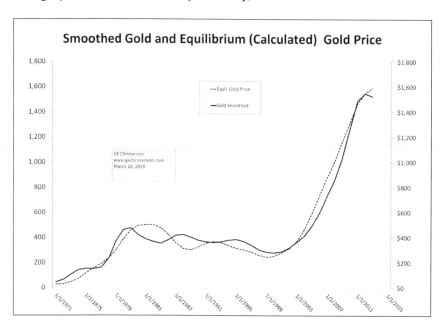

Potential prices for gold in 2017 and 2021 were listed as:

Year	Price	Possible Spike Highs
2017	$2,400 - $2,900	$3,500 - $4,500
2021	$4,000 - $5,000	$6,000 - $8,000

Of course the prices for gold will vary widely around the calculated Equilibrium Gold Price. We should expect that in the next ten years gold prices will experience several crashes and one blow-off bubble in which prices go parabolic for many months and astound everyone. If financial television is checking the price of gold every hour the bubble phase has arrived.

When comparing the prices of gold to the model, it appears that gold could easily move to new highs above $2,000 in 2014 - 2015 and perhaps to $3,500 or $4,000 within several years.

When comparing gold prices to the Dow Index, silver prices, and crude oil prices, there is no indication that gold is currently in a bubble or even in an over-bought condition when viewed from the perspective of several decades. Expect gold, silver, and crude oil prices to rise substantially.

It is clear to me that unless our current fiscal, monetary, and political systems change drastically, the national debt, price of crude oil, and the price of gold are headed much higher during the next decade. Obviously there are a number of conditions that could derail this analysis but they seem unlikely.

I encourage you to remember that digital and paper dollars are Federal Reserve Notes that function well for purchasing food, energy and housing. However they are less than satisfactory for preserving wealth. Over 5,000 years of history have demonstrated that gold is excellent at preserving wealth and purchasing power. I have little doubt that the next decade will confirm this ancient wisdom.

When you think about your savings, investments, wealth and retirement, consider:

1) The gold empirical model indicates much higher prices for gold are likely in the next decade.
2) History has shown that unbacked paper currency systems always fail.
3) Politicians and governments have been debasing their currencies for thousands of years with disastrous consequences. Politicians, governments, and central banks are now actively engaged in debasing their dollars, euros, yen and other currencies.
4) Expect governments and central banks of the world to continue devaluing their currencies.
5) Expect higher prices for everything you need, such as food, energy, and housing.
6) Expect taxes and consumer price inflation to increase.
7) Don't expect insolvent governments that survive only by increasing their indebtedness to increase, or even maintain, benefits to their citizens.
8) 5,000 years of history have shown that gold is a store of value.
9) Gold will remain after paper assets, paper currencies, and insolvent governments are gone.
10) We make decisions and experience the consequences of those decisions, so it behooves us to make the most informed and intelligent decisions possible. The gold empirical model is a valuable tool that can enhance our decision-making process.

I trust that the model and this book have increased your appreciation for the value of gold, your understanding of gold prices, and that it is clear gold prices will be higher in the relatively near future. Similarly I hope you have increased your skepticism toward our unbacked debt based currencies that appear to be self-destructing with the assistance of our central banks and governments.

My final comments: (See notes in Appendix One)

- Hemmingway: *"The first panacea of a mismanaged nation is inflation of the currency; the second is war."*
- We have been warned about "printing money," Quantitative Easing, and inflation.
- Printing money does not solve problems.
- Nothing was fixed after the 2008 crash. It can happen again.
- Our financial problems are structural, not cyclical.
- All bubbles eventually pop. By many measures sovereign debt and fiat currencies are bubbles. Gold is not currently in a bubble.
- The mathematics of debt and compound interest are difficult to refute.
- The price of gold can be considered the reciprocal of the world's faith in central banks.
- It will not end well.
- Choose wisely!

GE Christenson
April 2014

APPENDIX ONE: NOTES AND ADDITIONAL ANALYSIS:

Chapter 1 Notes:

GOLD AS WEALTH:

For hundreds of years an ounce of gold was just that – an ounce of gold – and, as chosen by most cultures, a significant amount of wealth or savings. A simple example is shown in the following table:

Gold	Comment	Approximate Value in 2014
1 oz.	1 - 2 week's work	$1,300
100 oz.	Middle class savings	$130,000
10,000 oz.	Upper class savings	$13,000,000
1,000,000 oz.	Massive wealth	$1,300,000,000

James Rickards was interviewed in March of 2014. In that interview he discussed manipulation of the gold price and future prices for gold. He stated:

> "Okay if we're going to have a new gold standard, what's the price? … and then did the math I described, that number today is about $9,000 an ounce."

David Marotta: "The Optimum Asset Allocation to Gold Is Always Zero"

"The optimum allocation to gold is always zero because its return is too low to be a real investment and its volatility is too high to justify its low return."

Note: I have included Mr. Marotta's comments as counterpoint to my views. He is certainly more traditional and mainstream in his thinking and he appears to represent Wall Street acceptable viewpoints regarding gold. Obviously, I disagree with the analysis and conclusions in his article in all material respects, but I think it is occasionally valuable to consider opposing viewpoints.

Mark J. Lundeen: The All Consuming Burdens of Debt

"Today, it would take $8750 current dollars to equal the same $30 in constant 1920 dollars (needed to purchase an ounce of gold in 1934 and in 1980) ..."

Mr. Lundeen has taken the price of gold and adjusted it for changes in "Currency in Circulation" since 1920. Although this does not take into account changes in population and possibly other issues, it does provide an interesting look at the price of gold for the past 90 years after that adjustment.

Chapter 8 Notes: Gold prices are managed and manipulated

Paul Craig Roberts and Dave Kranzier: "The Hows and Whys of Gold Price Manipulation"

> "The evidence of gold price manipulation is clear. In this article we present evidence and describe the process."

James Rickards regarding manipulation of the gold market:

> "The weight of evidence is clearly that the gold market is being very heavily manipulated."

Janet Tavokoli on "How to Corner the Gold Market"

> "First, let your greed overcome all regard for the stability of the global market, and overcome your aversion to illegal activities…"

James Rickards on March 24, 2014:

> "Central banks still have the ability to manipulate gold prices through gold leasing to commercial banks, which then use the leased gold to sell unallocated gold to customers using leverage."

GoldForecaster.com on December 20, 2013:

> "Gold price manipulation is a matter of history. It happened, it happens … But there are deeply troubling consequences on the way!"

The Gold Anti-Trust Action Committee (GATA) March 2014:

GATA quoted Zhang Jie, deputy editor of the Chinese publication Global Finance and a consultant to the China Gold Association. He made it clear that China understands that the Federal Reserve manipulates gold prices in order to protect the US dollar as the world reserve currency.

Chapter 10 Notes: Gold market cycles

Ron Rosen uses his "delta" cycle turning points. He stated in February 2014:

> **"At that time the precious metals complex should explode upward in a huge bullish move. Gold will probably triple in price from the low of $1,179.40."**

More analysis of future gold prices and timing via the golden ratio is discussed here: "**Gold Projection by the Golden Ratio**"

> *"This article shows how Gold has been following the Golden Ratio which predicted all the major turning points with a high degree of accuracy for the past thirty years…"*

Chapter 13 Notes: Counter-party risk

From Taki Tsaklanos: "Gold's Protection Against Counter-party Risk is Coming Alive"

"Gold's protection serves individuals as well as countries. The "Golden Rule" will continue to be relevant to countries: he who holds the gold rules. Quoting Michael Noonan: "The transition of physical gold from West to East is disrupting the elites' domination of the entire financial world. The East has been saying "Enough is enough." In our view, that is reflected in Eastern physical gold accumulation.

*To individuals, what matters is that **physical gold is immune to counter-party risk**. And this, ladies and gentlemen, we believe is the key take-away from the ongoing economic and financial turmoil. All those dollars, Treasuries, stocks, derivatives, i.e., running a risk to become the object of the new economic warfare, in the context of extreme leverage and excess liquidity, has one and only one antidote: unencumbered ownership of physical gold and silver."*

Chapter 14 Notes: The Fed, Interest Rates, QE and Inflation

The following articles were written by Taki Tsaklanos of goldsilverworlds.com

"Hyperinflation has struck already 56 times"

> "Nick Barisheff, CEO of Bullion Management Group Inc. and author of the book $10,000 Gold: Why Gold's Inevitable Rise Is the Investor's Safe Haven did a recent interview with Investor's Digest of Canada. In it, he explained how a hyperinflationary period does not occur by accident. It is rather a process which comes at the end of five stages. The pattern is recurring. This article covers the process which leads to hyperinflation and the answer to the question why Wall Street inclines to discredit the yellow metal."

"Mike Maloney: Expect First Real Deflation, Then Hyperinflation"

> "In this video, Mike Maloney is being asked where he sees the economy going in terms of inflation vs. deflation. To answer that question, he refers to the book he wrote about a decade ago, in which he wrote the following:
>
> **"First the threat of deflation, followed by a helicopter drop, followed by big inflation, followed by real deflation, and then followed by hyperinflation."**
>
> Why does Maloney think so? Because the gigantic expansion of base money (which is the monetary base as created by the US Fed and visible on its balance sheet) is being offset by a collapse of the other monetary aggregates, a trend started in 2008.

Furthermore, the deflation could be much, much worse than the ones the world experienced in the 30ies. Why? Because of the scale of the ongoing emergency measures. This scale is not clear to most people. These are truly emergency measures … for 4 years in a row. For the Chairman Mr. Bernanke coming out not willing to taper is an admission that the whole system is ready to crash again and that there is no recovery."

"This type of monetary measures cannot come without economic consequence."

Micro-Documentary: Weimar Inflation vs. USA Today

"In a short but powerful documentary of 6 minutes, our friends at FutureMoney Trends show the similarities between the hyperinflationary period in the Weimar Republic in 1923 / 1924, and the USA today. The similarities in the pre-hyperinflationary period appear to be striking! In a nutshell:

- *The national debt had risen to a point where it could not realistically be paid back.*
- *The war had cost more than expected.*
- *There was a high unemployment.*
- *Products and services increased in price, while production decreased significantly.*
- *The government's response was to provide liquidity to the banks and inflate the currency.*
- *The gold standard was left several years before."*

Research Shows ALL Paper Money Systems Failed

> *"The monetary environment we are living in, is a ticking time bomb...The figures are clear. ALL the 599 analyzed paper money systems did disappear."*

....

From Wikipedia listing previous hyperinflations:

Angola
Argentina
Armenia
Austria
Azerbaijan
Belarus
Bolivia
Bosnia and Herzegovina
Brazil
Bulgaria
Chile
China
Estonia
France
Free City of Danzig
Georgia
Germany (Weimar Republic)
Greece
Hungary, 1923–24
Hungary, 1945–46
Kazakhstan
Kyrgyzstan
Serbian Krajina
North Korea

Nicaragua

Peru

Philippines

Poland, 1923–1924

Poland, 1989–1990

Republika Srpska

Soviet Union / Russian Federation

Taiwan

Tajikistan

Turkmenistan

Ukraine

Uzbekistan

Yugoslavia

Zaire (now the Democratic Republic of the Congo)

Zimbabwe

Chapter 15 Notes: Central bank gold sales

From Eric Sprott: "Do Central Banks Have Any Gold Left???"

> "The conclusion we have reached is that this gold has been supplied by Central Banks, who have replaced their holdings of physical gold with claims on gold (paper gold)."

Robin Griffiths – "Historic Fed Decision's Impact on Gold and Major Markets"

> "Central banks have been trying to disrupt the bull move but they have simply ended up with nothing in their vaults."

From Bill Bonner: "Why Gold is the Only Money That Works**"**

> "A credit system cannot last in the modern world. Because, as the volume of credit rises, the creditworthiness of the issuers declines. The more they owe, the less able they are to pay."

But suppose much of the government and central bank gold is gone. As Eric Sprott concluded, after considerable research:

> **"Our analysis of the physical gold market shows that central banks have most likely been a massive unreported supplier of physical gold, and strongly implies that their gold reserves are negligible today."**

Bill Bonner:

> "But if they (central banks) have sold such massive quantities over the last 10 years, how much do they have left? Maybe not much."

Alan Greenspan (1993):

"Nor can private counterparties restrict supplies of gold, another commodity whose derivatives are often traded over-the-counter, where central banks stand ready to lease gold in increasing quantities should the price rise."

Chapter 16 Notes: How and when to purchase gold?

I have direct and indirect experience with many of these dealers and have no issues or complaints. Do your own due diligence.

American Bullion:	www.americanbullion.com
APMEX:	www.apmex.com
Bullion Management Group:	www.bmgbullion.com
Bullion Vault:	www.bullionvault.com
Global Gold:	www.globalgold.ch
GoldMoney:	www.goldmoney.com
GoldSilver.com:	www.goldsilver.com
Gold Switzerland:	www.goldswitzerland.com
Investment Rarities Inc.:	www.investmentrarities.com
Hard Assets Alliance:	www.hardassetsalliance.com
Houston Numismatic:	www.hnex.com
Lear Capital:	www.learcapital.com
Liberty Gold and Silver:	www.libertygoldandsilver.com
Merit Gold and Silver:	www.meritgold.com
Miles Franklin:	www.milesfranklin.com
Monex Precious Metals:	www.monex.com
Perth Mint:	www.perthmint.com.au
SilverSaver:	www.silversaver.com
Why Not Gold:	www.whynotgold.com
USA Gold:	www.usagold.com

Don't underestimate the value of allocated gold storage in a country other than the country in which you live. Many analysts believe Switzerland and Singapore offer attractive and safe storage options at a nominal cost.

Know your dealer and be careful. Occasionally a dealer steals from his clients and such news is widely distributed by the generally anti-gold media.

However there are many examples of other mainstream companies stealing from their clients, such as MFGlobal, several other brokerage firms, and a number of Ponzi schemes, the most notorious of which was the one operated by Mr. Bernie Madoff.

Again, know your dealer.

Conclusions Notes - We have been warned!

INFLATION, HYPERINFLATION AND QUANTITATIVE EASING:

From Richard Russell:

> "For the first time in history, ALL the major central banks are printing money. One of two things will occur. If they continue to print, their respective currencies will lose their purchasing power, and we'll have inflation or even hyper-inflation."

Hugo Salinas Price:

> "The world will plunge into the darkness of massive world inflation. There is no other alternative."

Jim Grant:

> "I think the odds against a painless, peaceful and placid exit from all of this dollar, yen, euro and pound sterling creation, the odds against returning to something like normalcy, are very slight indeed"

Arabian Money:

> "What you want to buy is an insurance policy against this coming catastrophe and preferably one that does not have a third party between you and your money. Gold is the ultimate money in times of chaos."

Egon von Greyerz:

"We are in the final stages of an era of extreme decadence, an era that sadly cannot and will not have a happy ending."

John Rubino: (on complexity)

"…when the system doubles in size, the instability goes up tenfold. It means as well that it requires an exponential amount of energy to keep the system growing."

Ernest Hemmingway:

"The first panacea for a mismanaged nation is inflation of the currency; the second is war."

David Stockman:

"I think the political realities of the situation make the most likely scenario one in which there will be some kind of real financial collapse and disorder that will require a total reconstruction of the system."

Egon von Greyerz:

"Why will the dollar go down? For the simple reason that the US has created a mountain of debt of enormous proportions…"

Bill Fleckenstein:

"Money-printing cannot solve problems. … What money-printing has accomplished is to push the stock market high *enough to cause people to once again become delusional in their expectations."*

Egon von Greyerz:

"Debt worldwide is now expanding exponentially. With absolutely no possibility of stopping this debt explosion, we will soon enter a period of unlimited money printing..."

Karl Denninger:

"There is a mathematically-certain collapse in our funding and economic model in the offing ..."

Vincent Cate:

"Hyperinflation happens when debt is over 80% of GNP and deficit is over 40% of government spending. The US is at or near these numbers, so the danger of hyperinflation is real."

Chris Martenson:

"How does all this end? Like it has every other time in history, with a final destruction of the currencies involved. That's my best guess."

Nick Barisheff:

"When you start looking at the history of currencies, there isn't one example in human history where fiat currency didn't go through a hyperinflation and complete collapse. Not one!"

John Rubino:

"The conditions for a global catastrophic failure are in place."

Steve Saville: (on Quantitative Easing)

"So, the Fed has done what we thought it would have enough sense not to do at this time."

Charles Hugh Smith described The Fed as "The World's Largest Money Laundering Machine."

"This thought experiment reveals the real agenda of the Fed's asset purchases: it's not about aiding the nation or borrowers, it's all about funneling "free money" to the banks to restore their balance sheets and profits."

Peter Schiff:

"Bernanke and his Wall Street supporters see cheap money until the horizon - but that horizon is really a painted brick wall. … the only way to get off this locomotive is to invest in hard assets."

Steve Saville:

"We've speculated in TSI commentaries that unwavering devotion to bad economic theory (a type of stupidity) is the most likely reason for the Fed's introduction of a new inflation program at this time."

Ron Paul:

"The American public now senses that the Fed's actions, especially since 2008, are enormously inflationary and will cause great harm to the American economy in the long run."

Hugo Salinas Price:

"The Chinese government knows that the dollar will not be around forever. China is purchasing enormous amounts of gold to add to their huge pile of US Bonds…"

CENTRAL BANKING:

Jim Grant:

"The price [of gold] is the reciprocal of the world's faith in central bankers. The world ought to have much less faith in central bankers."

Michael Noonan:

"If the paper "dollar" is how you measure your worth, you have been warned."

Bill Bonner:

"The feds decided to fight fire with fire. To solve the debt problem, they added debt! The genius of this plan was, we admit, not immediately obvious. …"

John Rubino:

> *"… nothing was fixed after 2008, just as nothing was fixed after the housing, tech stock, and junk bond bubbles burst. … With financial imbalances bigger than ever before – and continuing to expand – the only possible outcome is an even bigger crash."*

From Richard Russell: (subscription service)

> *"The compounding debt is the monster that is eating the U.S.. The only way out is to renege on the debt or try to pay it off with inflation or hyperinflation."*

From "The Burning Platform: Trying to Stay Sane in an Insane World – Part 1"**

> *"The immense forces of normalcy bias and social inertia have led millions to refuse to understand the mathematical certainty of the coming collapse."*

Ben Bernanke on November 21, 2002:

> *"U.S. dollars have value only to the extent that they are strictly limited in supply. But the U.S. government has a technology, called a printing press…"*

Wall Street Journal on September 2012: Five renowned economists published an editorial and said:

> *"The problems are close to being unmanageable now. If we stay on the current path, they will wind up being completely unmanageable, culminating in an unwelcome explosion and crisis."*

DEBT, BUBBLES, AND PONZI SCHEMES:

Bill Holter:

> "A war is necessary. It is necessary so that fingers can be pointed to it as the reason for all things bad…"

Michael Noonan:

> "Gold and Silver: From now on all that matters is that you own both."

Simon Black regarding Italian history:

> "And as one Emperor after another bankrupted the treasury through foreign wars, palatial opulence, and unaffordable social welfare programs, Rome gradually changed for the worse."

QUOTATIONS REGARDING GOLD AND GOVERNMENT:

Keynote Speech At Sydney Gold Symposium 14-15 November 2011 By Alf Field.

> "… the root cause of the GFC [global financial crisis] is unsound money created at will by governments, combined with a banking system that has enabled the creation of an unsustainable mountain of debt."

APPENDIX TWO: REFERENCES AND SOURCE INFORMATION

Chapter 1:

Jim Sinclair is a recognized expert regarding the gold markets. He has half a century of experience and a large number of loyal followers. He operates the website www.jsmineset.com.

Quotes from JP Morgan, Paul Volcker, Benjamin Bernanke, and Janet Yellen are widely referenced at various sites on the internet. Mr. Volcker, Mr. Bernanke, and Mrs. Yellen are former or current Chairpersons of the Federal Reserve Open Market Committee, otherwise known as "The Head of the Fed."

James Turk is the founder of www.goldmoney.com and the co-author of "The Collapse of the Dollar and How to Profit From It" with John Rubino. The link to his article is: http://www.fgmr.com/fear-index-rises-to-sixteen-year-high.html

Harry Dent: http://signups.survive-prosper.com/X195Q213

Robert Prechter: http://www.elliottwave.com/

David Marotta: http://www.emarotta.com/our-team/

Martin Armstrong: http://armstrongeconomics.com/armstrong_economics_blog/

James Rickards: http://jimrickards.blogspot.com/

Chapter 4

US National Debt: www.treasurydirect.gov

Chapter 8

Dimitri Speck: http://goldswitzerland.com/part-one-the-coordinated-effort-to-suppress-the-gold-price-dimitri-speck/ /

Nick Laird: http://www.sharelynx.com/

GATA: Gold Anti-Trust Action Committee: http://www.gata.org/

Ted Butler: http://www.butlerresearch.com/

Chapter 10

Ron Rosen: http://www.321gold.com/editorials/rosen/rosen020614.pdf

Golden Ratio: http://news.goldseek.com/GoldSeek/1395763563.php

Chapter 13

John Rubino: http://dollarcollapse.com/

Chapter 14:

Taki Tsaklanos:

> http://goldsilverworlds.com/gold-silver-insights/
> research-shows-all-paper-money-systems-failed/

Chapter 15

Alasdair MacLeod: http://www.goldmoney.com/research/analysis/
renewed-estimates-of-chinese-gold-demand

Chapter 18

James Rickards: "The Death of Money: The Coming Collapse of the International Monetary System," published by the Penguin Group, NY, NY

Notes Chapter 1:

James Rickards:

> http://www.sprottmoney.com/news/ask-the-expert-
> james-rickards-march-2014

David Martotta:

> http://www.marottaonmoney.com/the-optimum-
> asset-allocation-to-gold-is-always-zero/

Mark J. Lundeen:

> http://www.gold-eagle.com/article/all-consuming-
> burdens-debt

Notes Chapter 8:

Paul Craig Roberts:

http://www.paulcraigroberts.org/2014/01/17/
hows-whys-gold-price-manipulation/

James Rickards:

http://www.sprottmoney.com/news/ask-the-expert-
james-rickards-march-2014

Janet Tavokoli:

http://www.tavakolistructuredfinance.com/2010/03/
corner-gold-market/

Goldforecaster:

http://news.goldseek.com/GoldForecaster/1387573200.
php

GATA:

http://news.goldseek.com/GATA/1395846000.php

Notes Chapter 10:

Ron Rosen and the Delta Society

https://www.deltasociety.com/content/ron-rosen-
precious-metals-timing-letter

Ron Rosen:

> http://www.321gold.com/editorials/rosen/rosen020614.pdf

Golden Ratio:

> http://news.goldseek.com/GoldSeek/1395763563.php

Taki Tsaklanos:

> http://goldsilverworlds.com/money-currency/golds-protection-against-counterparty-risk-is-coming-alive/

> http://goldsilverworlds.com/money-currency/hyperinflation-has-struck-already-56-times-it-could-hit-again/

Notes Chapter 14:

> http://goldsilverworlds.com/money-currency/mike-maloney-expect-first-real-deflation-then-hyperinflation/

> http://goldsilverworlds.com/gold-silver-insights/micro-documentary-weimar-hyperinflation-1923-vs-usa-today/

> Wikipedia: http://en.wikipedia.org/wiki/Hyperinflation

Notes Chapter 15:

Eric Sprott:

> http://sprott.com/markets-at-a-glance/do-western-central-banks-have-any-gold-left-part-iii/

Robin Griffiths:

http://kingworldnews.com/kingworldnews/KWN_
DailyWeb/Entries/2013/9/18_Historic_Fed_Decisions_
Impact_On_Gold_%26_Major_Markets.html

Bill Bonner:

http://www.dailyreckoning.com.au/why-gold-is-the-
only-money-that-works/2013/07/23/

Eric Sprott:

http://www.sprott.com/markets-at-a-glance/do-
western-central-banks-have-any-gold-left/

Alan Greenspan:

http://www.gata.org/node/8208

Notes Conclusions:

Richard Russell:

http://www.financialsense.com/contributors/richard-
russell/is-something-ominous-in-cards

Hugo Salinas Price:

http://plata.com.mx/mplata/articulos/articlesFilt.
asp?fiidarticulo=222

Jim Grant:

http://kingworldnews.com/kingworldnews/KWN_
DailyWeb/Entries/2013/9/27_Jim_Grant_-_The_World_
Will_Witness_Extreme_Monetary_Disorder.html

Arabian Money:

http://www.arabianmoney.net/gold-silver/2013/09/28/
why-gold-will-be-the-standout-winner-from-the-next-
bout-of-chaos-in-financial-markets-hitting-7000-10000/

Egon von Greyerz:

http://goldswitzerland.com/the-real-state-of-the-world-
economy-is-dire/#more-12904

John Rubino:

http://goldsilverworlds.com/gold-silver-insights/john-
rubino-we-created-the-conditions-for-catastrophic-
failure/

David Stockman:

http://goldsilverworlds.com/economy/david-stockman-
collapse-lead-to-reconstruction-of-system/

Egon von Greyerz:

http://kingworldnews.com/kingworldnews/KWN_
DailyWeb/Entries/2013/9/20_Man_Who_Predicted_No_
Fed_Tapering_Now_Says_To_Expect_Chaos.html

Bill Fleckenstein:

> http://money.msn.com/bill-fleckenstein/post--
> is-the-end-of-an-error-coming-soon

Egon von Greyerz:

> http://kingworldnews.com/kingworldnews/KWN_
> DailyWeb/Entries/2013/9/13_Historic_JP_Morgan_
> Whistleblower_Interview_Moves_Markets.html

Karl Denninger:

> www.market-ticker.com

Vincent Cate:

> http://howfiatdies.blogspot.com/2012/08/mish-on-
> hyperinflation.html

Chris Martenson:

> http://news.goldseek.com/GoldSeek/1348067335.php

Nick Barisheff:

> http://goldsilverworlds.com/gold-silver-insights/why-
> mainstream-media-main-street-and-institutions-fail-to-
> see-the-benefits-of-gold/

John Rubino:

> http://dollarcollapse.com/long-wave/the-long-wave-
> versus-the-printing-press-central-banks-go-all-in/

Steve Saville:

> http://news.goldseek.com/SpeculativeInvestor/
> 1347975515.php

Charles Hugh Smith:

> http://oftwominds.com/blogoct12/Fed-money-
> laundering10-12.html

Peter Schiff:

> http://news.goldseek.com/GoldSeek/1349795100.php

Steve Saville:

> http://www.321gold.com/editorials/saville/saville092512.
> html

Ron Paul:

> http://news.goldseek.com/RonPaul/1342445100.php

Hugo Salinas Price:

> http://www.plata.com.mx/mplata/articulos/articlesFilt.
> asp?fiidarticulo=237

Jim Grant:

> http://www.moneynews.com/Markets/gold-
> banks-government-shutdown/2013/10/03/
> id/529049/

Michael Noonan:

http://www.gold-eagle.com/article/gold-and-silver-%E2%80%93-central-bank-death-dance-part-i

Bill Bonner:

http://www.bonnerandpartners.com/if-this-is-success-then-give-us-failure/#.U2K-W_ldXNt

John Rubino:

http://dollarcollapse.com/the-economy/mass-delusion-and-the-myth-of-deleveraging/

Richard Russell:

http://ww1.dowtheoryletters.com/

The Burning Platform:

http://theburningplatform.com/?p=57636

The Wall Street Journal:

http://online.wsj.com/news/articles/SB10001424052702303561504577497442109193610?mg=reno64-wsj&url=http%3A%2F%2Fonline.wsj.com%2Farticle%2FSB10001424052702303561504577497442109193610.html

Bill Holter:

http://blog.milesfranklin.com/when-no-war-is-bad

Michael Noonan:

http://goldsilverworlds.com/money-currency/gold-silver-from-now-on-all-that-matters-is-that-you-own-both/

Simon Black:

https://www.sovereignman.com/trends/you-need-to-be-in-front-of-this-trend-12628/

Alf Field:

http://www.jsmineset.com/2011/11/14/keynote-speech-at-sydney-gold-symposium-14-15-november-2011-by-alf-field/

ACKNOWLEDGEMENTS

I sincerely thank my wife for her support and assistance in writing this book, editing the text, acting as my sounding board, and encouraging me along the way.

I sincerely thank Taki Tsaklanos of www.goldsilverworlds.com for his editorial comments regarding content, structure, organization and emphasis. His assistance was invaluable.

ABOUT THE AUTHOR

GE Christenson is the owner and writer for the popular investment site www.deviantinvestor.com.

He is a retired accountant and business manager with 30 years of experience studying markets, investing, and trading.

Many years ago he did graduate work in physics. He currently lives in Granbury, Texas with his wife.

INDEX

15030072R00090

Made in the USA
San Bernardino, CA
12 September 2014